PROBLEMS OF SOCIETY

AN ESOTERIC VIEW

From Luciferic Past to Ahrimanic Future

D1610730

PROBLEMS OF SOCIETY
AN ESOTERIC VIEW

From Luciferic Past to Ahrimanic Future

Ten lectures held in Zurich, Bern, Heidenheim and Berlin between 4 February and
4 November 1919

TRANSLATED BY MATTHEW BARTON

INTRODUCTION BY MATTHEW BARTON

RUDOLF STEINER

RUDOLF STEINER PRESS

CW 193

The publishers gratefully acknowledge the generous funding of this publication by the estate of Dr Eva Frommer MD (1927–2004) and the Anthroposophical Society in Great Britain

Rudolf Steiner Press
Hillside House, The Square
Forest Row, RH18 5ES

www.rudolfsteinerpress.com

Published by Rudolf Steiner Press 2015

Originally published in German under the title *Der innere Aspekt des sozialen Rätsels* (volume 193 in the *Rudolf Steiner Gesamtausgabe* or Collected Works) by Rudolf Steiner Verlag, Dornach. Based on shorthand transcripts and notes, not reviewed by the speaker. This authorized translation is based on the latest available (fifth) edition of 2007 edited by Hendrik Knobel and Urs Dietler

Published by permission of the Rudolf Steiner Nachlassverwaltung, Dornach

A catalogue record for this book is available from the British Library

ISBN 978 1 85584 516 9

Cover by Mary Giddens
Typeset by DP Photosetting, Neath, West Glamorgan
Printed and bound by Gutenberg Press Ltd., Malta

CONTENTS

LECTURE 1
ZURICH, 4 FEBRUARY 1919

The human being as the centre of the universe. Cultural life as ideological shadow, and devotion to the spirit. The relation of the human soul to spiritual beings and to other human beings in the past and now. Becoming mature by learning throughout life. Spiritual insights into the child in later life, and their social importance.

LECTURE 2
BERN, 8 FEBRUARY 1919

The social question as a problem for all humanity. Disparity between the proletarian, materialistic outlook and that of spiritual science. The structure of earthly culture. The external state. Economic life. Totemism. Social powers shaping the medieval Church. The paralysis of spiritual culture as sin of modern times.

LECTURE 3
ZURICH, 11 FEBRUARY 1919

Earthly culture and pre-birth existence. The political state as an expression of purely earthly impulses. Economic impulses point us towards after-death existence. Nationalism as retrograde tendency and the meaning of the Christ impulse. Yahweh and Christ in modern theology. The path of thinking and the path of the will towards Christ. Supersensible responsibility towards all things.

Anglo-American peoples. Freeing modern commercial life from Greek cultural life and the Roman state. The spiritual battles between East and West.

LECTURE 8

BERLIN, 14 SEPTEMBER 1919

The human being's complete immersion in the body. The need to develop scientific ideas. The new ideals of education. Differences in understanding of the Christ event. Woodrow Wilson and the League of Nations. The new understanding of Christ. The human being's importance for the life of the earth and the world of spirit. Temptations in West and East. Rabindranath Tagore. Pie-in-the-sky thinking amongst leading individuals during the First World War. Ludendorff, Michaelis. The will for truth.

LECTURE 9

ZURICH, 27 OCTOBER 1919

The ancient wisdom of heathen peoples and the world-view of the Jewish people. The incarnation of Lucifer at the beginning of the third millennium BC. The primal wisdom of the third post-Atlantean era, ancient Greece, and the Gnosis. Theology becomes materialistic. The incarnation of Ahriman. Deceptions of which Ahriman makes use as he prepares to incarnate. Cardinal Newman. The Lux Mundi movement. The meaning of the divergence between the four Gospels.

LECTURE 10

BERN, 4 NOVEMBER 1919

Heathen and Jewish culture. The incarnation of Lucifer at the beginning of the third millennium BC. More detailed account of Lucifer's incarnation. Luciferic wisdom as the foundation of Greek culture and the Gnosis. The incarnation of Ahriman in the West. The means employed by Ahriman to prepare his incarnation. Cardinal Newman. Robert Willbrandt. Intellect and spiritual experience. The spirit sustaining us as the physical body decays.

EDITOR'S PREFACE

In 1919, a year marked by strong social and political upheavals, Rudolf Steiner was deeply concerned with questions about society. Four lectures given in Zurich in February of that year formed the basis for his book *Towards Social Renewal* (GA 23), which was published (in German) in April in an edition of 40,000 copies. The idea of the threefold social organism, and thoughts about realizing it in practice, were publicized in a big campaign.

Besides the public lectures on threefolding, Rudolf Steiner also gave more in-depth lectures on this subject for members of the Anthroposophical Society, in efforts to kindle their urgently needed enthusiasm for this concern. The lectures compiled in this volume should be read and understood very much as Marie Steiner stressed in the title 'The Inner Aspect of the Social Question' which she gave to the first edition of the members' lectures in Zurich that form part of this compilation: as a complement to very practical efforts to realize threefolding in the historical context of that time.

INTRODUCTION

What is society? Margaret Thatcher famously said 'there is no such thing', though in fact she went on to qualify (or perhaps exacerbate) this much-derided statement by saying: 'It's our duty to look after ourselves, and then also to look after our neighbour.'[*] In that order, clearly, and probably a little grudgingly. This seemingly rational idea—that we put ourselves first before considering others—is a persuasive notion, a dangerous half-truth far more toxic therefore than an outright lie. 'Charity begins at home' is a formulaic and vacuous phrase which pays only secondary lip-service to the needs of others. As becomes very clear in these lectures, everything and everyone in the world is, or could be, precious to us if we enlarge our imaginative scope to find ourselves in the other. In a sense we *are* the other, our small, separate self enlarged by this encompassing gesture. It is not a matter of caring for ourselves *first*, and *then* seeing what others need, but of recognizing how we are all simultaneously connected, and that the boundaries between I and thou are, literally, self-created.

Steiner urges us to realize that the lack that another suffers diminishes us. This thought, expressed in numerous ways and with diverse but recurring emphasis, is the ground-tone of this series of lectures. We connect with our own highest being—the Christ—not by encircling ourselves with self-interested defences, whether in small cliques, or on a larger scale, for example in 'Fortress Europe', but by slowly developing beyond arid ideologies to create social community that is also a spiritual reality. Anything else is to live and perpetuate a kind of lie. Such community in the broadest sense widens beyond our

---

[*] In an interview published in *Women's Own* Magazine on 31 October 1987.

affiliations of race and nation to include not only the rest of humanity but the other kingdoms of nature and the invisible spiritual realms which inform physical reality. Economics, as Steiner makes plain, is or could be the practice of fraternity, whereas mostly, because it exceeds its proper scope, it is employed instead to cement unjust divisions.

But in a telling image Steiner also reminds us that it is not enough to spout these well-meaning ideas unless, at the same time, we are active in working for change that does, certainly, begin with each one of us separately, our own narrow perceptions, outlooks and self-interest. Commanding a stove to get hot will achieve nothing, he says. What is needed of course is to fill it with kindling and strike a match. While the ways Steiner suggests this can be done will not seem self-evident to a 'pragmatist', they will nevertheless strike a resonant chord in many who seek deeper answers to the social misery of our times, which pragmatism of any political persuasion has so far failed to remedy. The current refugee crisis in Europe has perhaps begun to show us that where politicians fail to cope with reality through abstract measures, some citizens are ahead of the game, opening their hearts and homes to the 'others' streaming into their country and acknowledging their own full, human responsibility.

Time and again in these lectures, Steiner urges us to turn away from 'fixed principles, theories or social dogmas', appealing instead to the intrinsic nature of the human being as the only reality on which society can be founded. But this reality cannot be understood in materialistic or deterministic ways. 'Whatever turbulent outward events occur in the world', says Steiner in lecture 5 in this volume, 'whatever form is taken by things seeking to work their way out of the underdepths of human evolution, we only really hearken to the true, underlying nature of these events—which escapes the notice of ordinary human perception—if we observe the world from a spiritual perspective.' Almost a hundred years after those words were spoken, the world still faces tumultuous events that will not be solved by desperate measures of 'practical' containment such as the closing of European borders and their encirclement in razor wire. Whatever the immediate causes of such huge and desperate upheavals, the underdepths of evolution are asking a great deal more of us, surely, than stop-gap or quick-fix solutions.

Matthew Barton, September 2015

LECTURE 1

ZURICH, 4 FEBRUARY 1919

SINCE I am giving public lectures here on the social question,[1] it may be a good idea for us in these branch evenings[2] to consider more inward aspects of the riddle of society, which is of such importance and concern today.

Whenever we meet another person, perceive him with our body-bound faculties of perception and feeling, we must of course acknowledge his intrinsic, deeper-lying inner nature. We can only perceive this more inward reality of a person when we realize that basically it is connected with everything that streams and weaves through the world as we experience it, informing our whole life. Our anthroposophic world-view is really very different from ordinary views of the world. If you take a look at my *Occult Science*, where I attempted to summarize this anthroposophic view of the world, you will find that not only is our nature connected with evolution on earth, but this earth itself has emerged from former planetary embodiments: from Moon evolution, which in turn proceeded from Sun evolution, and this, again, from Saturn evolution. But if we study these larger contexts and trace these great spans of evolution right up to our current developmental stage, we also find that the human being is intrinsic to them, is everywhere present. We regard the whole cosmos with all its forces and with everything that occurs in it as intrinsically related to the human being. The human being, in this view, stands at the centre of the cosmos.

In one of my Mystery Plays,[3] in a conversation between Capesius and the initiate, I gave special emphasis to this foundation of our whole anthroposophic world-view and its relationship to human sensibility—the impression it inevitably makes on us when we see that all generations of the gods, all forces in the cosmos have ultimately been invoked to create us, to place us at the centre of Creation.

At the same time I have stressed the great need for humility, specifically in relation to this absolutely true idea. We have to keep reminding ourselves that if we were actually able to manifest our whole being, living in and around us as we lead our lives on earth, if we were able to experience and realize this being, we would embody a microcosm of the whole of the rest of the world. But how much of it can we experience, how much can we manifest of what we are as human beings in the loftiest sense? When we realize what we human beings actually are, we can find ourselves fluctuating between feelings of humility and arrogance. Certainly we should not puff ourselves up in pride, but nor should we let ourselves dwindle into abject insignificance. We would do so if we did not set our sights as high as possible, our human task, remembering our true nature as an all-encompassing world-view discloses it. Basically, we can never have lofty enough ambitions about what we should be. We can never sufficiently prize the deeper, cosmic feeling of human responsibility that comes over us when we consider that the whole universe is centred upon our human nature.

But rather than remaining a more theoretical idea, in an anthroposophically oriented science of the spirit this should become a feeling, a sense of holy awe towards what we should be as human beings and yet can scarcely ever be. And when we meet another person, we should often have a sense that they bring something to expression in this present incarnation. There they stand, and, passing from one incarnation to another, a quality of the infinite informs the succession of their lives. There are other ways too in which we can broaden and deepen such feelings. Founded on a science of the spirit, this feeling gives rise to a proper sense of the value of humankind, a sense of the dignity of the human being. This feeling can fill our whole soul, expanding fully within us, and this alone will imbue us with the right mood in our individual dealings with other people. The mood I have here described is one we can regard as a first, essential achievement of a modern anthroposophically oriented spiritual science: a proper estimation of humanity in the world. That is the first thing.

A second thing will emerge from a preoccupation with anthroposophic spiritual science in so far as this develops real qualities of soul rather than remaining abstract and intellectual. And it is this. As we encompass all phenomena in the world, the elements of earth, water and air, everything shining down to us from the stars, the breezes that blow, everything conveyed to us by the different realms of nature, an anthroposophic outlook shows these to be related to us in some way. And everything becomes valuable to us, precious, as we relate it to ourselves in a certain way. A feeling relationship forms as we develop a supersensible perception of all things. The poet Christian Morgenstern[4] has expressed this feeling in some beautiful verses, as I have often mentioned when discussing a particular section of the Gospel of St John[5]—a feeling that comes over us when we allow the ascending realms of nature to work upon our sensibility. We see that the plant must inevitably feel itself to be higher in the hierarchy of life than merely lifeless minerals that give it the soil in which it roots. But it will say this: 'Though I am a higher entity than you, I grow forth from you and owe you my existence. In gratitude I bow before what is lower than I am.' The same quality again is one we must feel to exist in the relationship between animal and plant, and likewise in the human kingdom, the human being having ascended to a higher level in the sequence of his evolution. With reverence and respect he must look back to what in some senses is lower than he is, doing so not in a merely abstract, conceptual way, but really embodying and experiencing in his soul, as a cosmic feeling, all that pulses, lives and creates in all things. This is where the real essence of anthroposophic spiritual science leads us: it gives us the capacity to form a living human relationship with all other things.

And then there is a third thing. What spiritual science tells us of the spirit is not vague, pantheistic talk of spirit and yet more spirit underlying all things. No, this spiritual science does not merely *speak of* the real spirit but seeks to speak *out* of reality, from the spirit itself. Someone who lives in spiritual science knows that as thoughts of the spirit form in him it is the spirit itself that lives actively in these thoughts. Someone touched, if you like, by the breath of spiritual science, does not wish to express mere thoughts about the spirit but to let the spirit utter itself through his thoughts. The unmediated presence of the spirit, the active power of the spirit are what spiritual science seeks.

But now let us compare what is implanted in our inmost being of soul through a living involvement in spiritual science with what I spoke about yesterday:[6] the social demands emerging over time and living in a particular way in 'proletarian' consciousness as modern requirements in society. Consider what lives in this proletarian consciousness today and in a sense provides the basis of its percep-tions: an ideology, a mere fabric of abstract ideas. Nowadays in fact it is thought that all soul-spiritual experiences are, in essence, founded on merely commercial and economic factors, which alone are seen as real. The human being is considered to stand in a context of eco-nomic factors in which his struggle for survival unfolds. From these factors arises and emerges, like smoke and mist, all that he thinks and perceives; all that manifests in his art, all that he regards as ethics and morality, as law and justice and so on—all these things are seen as ideological shadows. Comparing this shadowy life of spirit, as it is thought to be, with the life of spirit that seeks to enter our souls from an anthroposophically oriented science of the spirit, we find that the latter, via the human soul, tries to place the spirit itself into the world as a living reality. The modern world-view, rooted in middle-class perceptions and then, disastrously, adopted by the proletariat, has banished the spirit, has no place for it. And so the spirit that should live in people as awareness of living, creative reality now leads only a shadowy existence as mere ideology.

How much of the deeper reality of human life, whose whole

context we see only by looking back before earth evolution to Moon, Sun and Saturn stages, is contained in this narrow view of earthly life perceived only through the senses, through our ordinary bodily perceptions? The realities of human existence fade from this modern consciousness. Only anthroposophic spiritual science gives us a true sense and feeling of human dignity, enabling us to find a proper relationship with others whom we encounter, as one individual meeting another. Is it actually conceivable in the present chaos of human society that people can find a proper relationship with each other, one which in turn offers the only real foundation for solving the conundrums of society? Can a mutual recognition of one another's rights actually emerge unless founded on a cosmic sense of human dignity that springs only from sources of spiritual perception and spiritual feeling?

In our relationship to the external world we ought not to seek abstract thoughts as economics and sociology do, but develop direct, personal connections with the diverse realities of the world. As far as outer human circumstances are concerned, we have to establish a real relationship to this world. Through anthroposophic spiritual science, we have to develop the inner feeling and sensibility I referred to above towards all non-human creatures and entities, towards everything that stands both below and above us in the hierarchies of nature and the divine order.

Now let us consider two things here: on the one hand the pro-letarian consciousness I spoke of, whose intellectual apprehensions are alienated to a very great degree from a sense of the living spirit at work in human beings and instead turn all spiritual life into ideology. If you picture how the modern proletarian thinks and in particular feels about his fellow men, and how this outlook informs his views, you will realize how very far removed this is from an estimation of the human being that fully comprehends the spirit. Consider also how far removed, ultimately, is the purely economic value of things—which has become more or less the only thing of importance for people nowadays—from the values we learn to invest in non-human creatures and entities through our deeper relationship to them, as I expressed this in terms of anthroposophically oriented spiritual science.

Here we have two different things: on the one hand the condition which the unspiritual nature of recent centuries has bred in humanity, affecting human souls to a very marked degree; and on the other, the hopes that can awaken at the prospect that a true science of the spirit can today enter humanity. If we put these two things side by side, it becomes apparent, surely, that in a human soul really imbued with what spiritual science can give it the right light will be shed on the riddle of society. If you bring the right sensibility to bear on these two perspectives—one hopeless, the other hopeful—then your work on behalf of anthroposophically oriented spiritual science will become what it needs to be for humanity today: an existential necessity which should pervade all other work and creativity.

No doubt you will say that nothing appears more comprehensible in the whole context of humanity's recent development than the emergence of the social problems that beset us, and that at the same time there is nothing more comprehensible than people's sense of helplessness before these problems. You see, at the very time that these social ills are knocking so audibly at the doorway of our understanding, of our views of the world, humanity is also passing through one of its severest trials: the need to turn towards the spirit through each person's inmost strength. Nowadays no revelations will be vouchsafed to us if we do not ourselves seek them in freedom, for since the middle of the fifteenth century we have been living in the era of the consciousness soul in which everything must be drawn into the light of awareness. There is no point lamenting the 'terrible catastrophe' that has broken over humanity or asking why the gods have allowed this to happen. There is no point in asking why the gods do not lead us safely out of this situation in which humanity finds itself so pitifully ensnared. Instead we must remember that we live in an age when inner human freedom must unfold and manifest, in an age when the gods may not reveal their most intrinsic intentions to us except in so far as we approach them by our own free resolve, willingly accepting them into our inmost soul.

We stand at a turning point today in relation to the most vital aspects of human evolution, in relation also to Christianity. There are individuals working in the social field today who gladly accept Christianity yet draw from it only as much as they can relate to their own social ideals. But this is not the way to integrate this impulse of core importance, this impulse which gives all earthly reality its true meaning and purpose. We have to realize that Christianity has so far only just begun to be embodied and expressed in humanity. Little more of Christianity has so far come to expression than human feelings in respect of the Mystery of Golgotha, apprehensions that Christ once lived on earth in the human being Jesus, and passed through the Mystery of Golgotha. In a sense these first two thousand years of Christianity on the earth have achieved little more—since human understanding has not yet ripened sufficiently—than to make it apparent for human awareness that Christ connected himself with the earth, that he descended to the earth. Only now, in the fifth post-Atlantean epoch, that of consciousness soul development, will humanity become mature enough not only to understand that Christ passed through the Mystery of Golgotha but also what actually lives in this Mystery. Humanity will only come to understand the content of this Mystery of Golgotha through the spiritual foundations that can develop during this fifth post-Atlantean era.

Here in these branch meetings I have frequently said how trivial it is for people to say that we 'live in a time of transition'. All times are transitional! We need to identify what each particular transition consists of. What is changing or transforming? I have characterized the major changes now occurring in human consciousness and human soul development from many different perspectives. Today, again from one specific angle, I would like to describe changes occurring in human evolution on earth in our particular time.

As I said a few moments ago, we try not only to formulate thoughts about the spirit in our anthroposophic spiritual science but seek, rather, for the reality of the spirit, seek thoughts in which the spirit itself lives and in which the spirit manifests. We can put it like this, too: Christ Jesus spoke these words, 'I am with you always, even unto the end of the world.'[7] While the Gospels are not the sole, exhaustive source of Christianity's content, we can acknowledge the truths of anthroposophic spiritual science by realizing that Christ really is here, and will remain with us always to the end of earthly times: not just as a finite power we are obliged to believe in, but as a living power that continually reveals more of itself. And what is this power revealing in our times? It reveals the content of modern anthroposophically oriented spiritual science, which seeks not only to speak *of* Christ but to express what Christ is at present trying to tell us through human thoughts.

In ancient times, when humankind still lived a more instinctual existence, and the human soul possessed something of an atavistic clairvoyance, this soul gave expression to spirit: spirit lived in human thoughts and in the human will. The gods then lived in human beings. Today they do so still, albeit in a rather different way from ancient times when the gods were pursuing a particular divine task in the form of earthly evolution. They attained this goal by inspiring human beings with their powers, endowing the human soul with imaginations. However strange it may sound to you, the divine worlds achieved and fulfilled their most intrinsic aims for earthly evolution, doing so, basically, by the end of the fourth post-Atlantean epoch. For this reason the spiritual beings of the higher hierarchies, whom we call the gods, now have a different relationship to the human soul than they did formerly. In ancient times the gods sought out human beings to realize their goals on earth with their aid. Today, by contrast, *we* must seek the gods, must raise ourselves to them out of our inmost impulse. Today we must seek to realize our aims, our conscious aims, with the help of divine powers. This is the fitting stance for people from the age of the consciousness soul onwards. In former times human aims were unconscious, instinctive, because divine aims lived within them. Human aims must now become ever more conscious, thus possessing powers that raise these aims to the gods and enable us to seek fulfilment of human aims with the aid of divine powers.

Think these words through carefully, for they are of great

importance. These words express a need for us to embark upon an original, elementary striving out of ourselves, which we can seek in diverse realms of the soul, above all at a deeper social level. Here we must consider interpersonal relations from a more spiritual-scientific perspective. In ancient times human beings rightly stood in far closer relation to each other by virtue of the fact that gods were realizing their aims in human evolution. Today people are in a sense driven asunder, and have to seek and reconnect with each other in a quite different way. People still need to learn how to do this. Even superficial observation can show this to be the case everywhere. Nowadays people know little about each other. In its cosmic apprehension of human dignity and human nature, spiritual science is as yet only in its infancy. People do not generally penetrate to the depths of each other's soul, but this is what must be found in a deeper social organism: new insight into human nature must enter human evolution.

But since the prevailing outlook today, devoid of spirit as it is, sees the human being only in terms of flesh and blood, we need to start perceiving the activity of gods in other human beings if we are to forge a really spirit-filled social organism. And this will only happen if we ourselves do something about it. One thing we can do here is to seek a certain deepening of our own life of soul. There are many ways to do this. I will only outline one meditative path here. We can look back on our life for all sorts of reasons, asking ourselves how we have developed as an individual from childhood onwards. But rather than focusing primarily on our own experiences, joys and sorrows, we can consider the people who affected us in some way as parents, siblings, friends, teachers and so on. Instead of placing ourselves at the centre of our thoughts, we can place there those who intervened in our life in some way. Then we will find, for a while at least, that our self has developed far less, really, from what we ourselves possessed and much more from what flowed into us from others. If we honestly and vividly picture this in a review of our life, our relationship to the world will actually become quite different. This review will leave us with feelings that act as germinal seeds in us, seeds of real insight into human nature. Someone who repeatedly examines himself and his life with a view to perceiving the part played in it by others, who may have died long ago or are now no longer close to him, will approach other people and form individual relationships with them in a way that allows an imagination to rise up in him of the true being of this other person. This is necessary, now and in the future, as an inner social requirement for human development. In this way anthroposophic spiritual science must become eminently practical in a way that engenders life and makes it fruitful.

I would like to offer one further perspective. In former times all self-knowledge, all self-reflection and observation of one's own soul was relatively easier, a good deal easier than it now is. And this is because a profoundly inward social impulse is now emerging—not just in relation to people's awareness of relative poverty or wealth—which comes to expression in the following way for instance. Nowadays we take little account of continuing maturation throughout a human life. Inwardly authentic people such as Goethe still felt this ever-developing maturity. Even in advanced old age, Goethe wished to go on learning, knowing that he was still not all that he could become. He looked back to his youth and young adulthood and saw that all that had occurred then was a preparation for what he could now experience in old age. People today scarcely think like this, especially when they consider people as social beings. Today everyone thinks he is ready to be a public servant at the age of 20 and make 'democratic' decisions. There is little awareness that we develop as life progresses and we mature towards old age. People do not think of this. That is one thing we have to relearn—that the whole compass of life brings us something, and not just the first two to three decades.

And then there is something else we need to learn. Besides considering ourselves we look around us at people of differing ages, above all the child who enters life at birth. In the same way as human evolution on earth was once instinctive, a 'given', but is now no longer so, things that formerly arose by themselves and became manifest in the human soul are now only available through our extreme exertions and efforts to gain supersensible knowledge, or at least real knowledge of life. As for humankind in general, much that belongs intrinsically to the child's nature remains hidden from him. Yet it is not only what the child will come to perceive as he matures towards old age that initially remains hidden from him, but a great deal else that was revealed in the past to humanity in ancient, instinctive times when people still possessed an atavistic clairvoyance. This too remains hidden from us if we reflect only upon ourselves. Between the cradle and the grave there is something that cannot reveal itself if we only seek knowledge within ourselves, and this is one of the peculiarities of the consciousness soul age. We can seek clarity of consciousness, but much in the field of vision that this clarity should illumine in fact remains concealed. This is a peculiarity of our times. In childhood we enter the world and there is something in us that is important for this world, for humanity's social relationships, for historical insights. But we fail to discern this if we seek no further than ourselves, whether as child, man, woman or in advanced age. But it can be perceived in another way if our mature human soul, as man, woman or old person, is more finely tuned through real spiritual sensibility and then considers the child. Then it can become apparent that something is revealed in the child that the child himself cannot discern, and will never be able to by his own devices however long he lives, but which can be discerned in another's soul when the latter, in old age, looks back to this child. Then there is something that can be revealed *through* the child: not *in* the child himself, and not in the man or woman into whom this child develops, but in another who looks back lovingly from advanced age to the earliest life of this child.

I indicate this especially, because in such a characteristic of our times you can discern the social impulse, in the broadest sense, that flows through our age. Surely a profoundly social trait is implicit in this necessity for something fruitful to enter life solely by virtue of the fact that an old person learns from an infant to co-exist for the highest good: not just any person with any other, but specifically an old person with an infant.

This social coexistence is something that shows us the inmost spirit and meaning of our age. Anthroposophic spiritual science can disclose such things to people whose familiarity with other aspects of spiritual science has prepared them to study deeper aspects of the social problem. All of you face a social task of great dimensions if you are to draw on the social sensibility we can kindle here to benefit modern humanity. You are especially fitted to do so through anthroposophically oriented spiritual science. In the context of current debate on issues of social co-existence and socialism you can try to kindle a deeper social sense, a deeper understanding of human relations. If you succeed in doing this you will be drawing on anthroposophy to fulfil a vital social task.

Next week we will speak further of these matters in the branch lecture between the two public lectures.

LECTURE 2

BERN, 8 FEBRUARY 1919

THE public lectures[8] I have been giving deal with the social problem, the social needs of today, not just as a theoretical appraisal shows them to be but as they actually manifest in the realities and occurrences of modern life in the world.

Anthroposophy can shed further light on all these things relating to human life, which nowadays require reflection of the broadest possible kind and in the widest possible circles. If we feel ourselves to be part of the anthroposophic movement, we ought never to forget the vital importance of considering everything in the world, all outward phenomena, as something requiring further penetration by insights drawn from the world of spirit. Everything acquires its proper aspect of reality only when we are able to conceive it as pervaded by spirit, by an essence which is initially invisible within the external earthly world but which nevertheless really does live in this world.

When I was here with you last time, I made some remarks from an anthroposophic perspective about the social impulses at work in human life.[9] We were trying to consider the human being as a social being, with both social and anti-social instincts. But we must never overlook the fact that as earthly human beings we introduce into earthly life effects that are the outcome of experiences we have between death and a new birth. Into each life we lead here we bring the fruits of our previous sojourn in worlds of spirit, in a purely supersensible world. And in fact we cannot fully comprehend this earthly life of ours if we do not remember that whatever we do here, what occurs here in the world in our coexistence with others, at the same time bears something of the signature of effects brought about by our life in the world of spirit, from which we emerge at birth and whose traces and powers we bring with us into this life.

On the one hand we have here what originates in the world of spirit for us and informs our life in the physical world. But there is another aspect too: in the life we lead on earth things happen that we are not initially fully conscious of, that happen to us and around us without us taking real cognizance of them. And yet it is these experiences particularly, which remain in our subconscious during life between birth and death, which are of the utmost importance when we carry them with us through the portal of death into the supersensible world, leaving the earthly world again. There are many things that happen during our life on earth that are not of direct importance for this life itself but instead are significant as preparation for our life after death. I am making a distinction here, therefore, between 'life before birth' and 'life after death'.

My reflections in yesterday's public lecture are of a kind that only come to full and detailed clarity if we also know how to illumine them with the light drawn from the supersensible world. Today therefore I want to study this highly topical theme in more depth with the help of anthroposophic insights. I wish to consider the social problem as a problem of all humanity. However, humanity in its totality is for us not just the sum of souls who are living at any one time in social coexistence upon the earth, but also includes those who, at the same time, are living in the supersensible world, for they are connected by spiritual bonds to those on earth, and together they form the full scope of humanity. Let us therefore first reflect on what we call human culture in an earthly sense, the life of the human spirit.

In its earthly meaning, human culture or spiritual life is not the life of spiritual beings but something humankind experiences together in its social coexistence. This cultural life includes, above all, everything that encompasses science, art and religion. At the same time it likewise includes everything that relates to schooling and education. We will therefore first consider what human beings experience as cultural life in their social coexistence. From what I said yesterday you will have gathered that this life of the human spirit—all schooling, education, all science, art, literary life and so forth—must take shape in its own distinct sphere of society. To make clear to the outer world why this is so we have to formulate it in ways that this outer world itself can accept. It is clear that healthy human common sense has to be sufficient to fully fathom these things, although we can only gain a really tangible sense of them if we embrace an anthroposophic view of the world. If we do, then what is called human culture appears in a very distinctive light.

Modern developments have led this cultural life to fall under the sway of an intellectual bourgeoisie and become diluted into mere ideology. The proletariat have adopted this schematic ideology into their world-view, in which all the realms I listed above arise simply from economic factors. The proletarian world-view today pictures things roughly in the following terms: all religious conviction and religious ideas, all artistic accomplishments, all views of justice and morality are, they say, a superstructure, something like a spiritual puff of smoke that ascends from the only true reality, that of economics. In these terms human culture on earth becomes mere ideology, something that is simply conceived intellectually. But for someone acquainted with the foundations on which anthroposophically oriented spiritual science originates, the cultural and spiritual life in which human beings are embedded is a gift of beings of spirit themselves. In this view it does not simply rise up like mist from underground economic factors, but streams down instead from the life of the spiritual hierarchies. An intellectual view of the world, developing from the fifteenth and sixteenth centuries, and its legacy in the proletarian outlook, according to which the spiritual world is an ideological construct, a vaporous emanation from harmonious and disharmonious economic factors, is radically different from the world-view that must now make headway, which alone will bring healing and lead us out of the chaos of modern life. In this outlook, we can draw on the world's true life of spirit which descends to us, streams down upon us. We belong to this world just as fully as we belong to the earthly, physical world through our senses and rational mind. And now, in the fifth post-Atlantean epoch, we can only find our way into the human social organism as social beings, can only embed this life of spirit there, because of preparations we undertake for this earthly human culture before birth, before we descended to earthly existence, entering there into relationship with other spirit beings of the hierarchies, as we have often described.

At birth we enter into relationship with other human beings in two ways, and it is important to distinguish these clearly. One of these is to do with our destiny connections with others. We are drawn to one person or another, to a larger or smaller number of people in a destined context. Entering earthly existence at birth, we come to a particular family, to father, mother, siblings and the wider family around us. This is given as our destiny.

We also enter as individuals into destined connections with other individuals, living out the karma we have with them. How does this karma arise? How do these connections of destiny come about? They arise, or were prepared, by factors and circumstances that existed in our previous life on earth. Let's be clear about this: through birth you enter into relationship with others, you connect as one individual with other individuals and live out the destiny that corresponds to your life with these individuals in previous lives on earth. This is one way in which you enter into relationships with others—through destined connections.

But you develop other relationships too. You belong to a group of people who together form a nation, and you are not connected with all of them by destiny. You are born into a particular race and nation, into a particular territory as it were. No doubt this is also to do with your karma, yet at the same time it means that you are forged into a social organism with many others to whom you do not intrinsically belong by destiny. In a religious community, too, you may share the same religious feelings or sensibility with many others with whom, however, you do not have a common destiny at all. Cultural life on earth creates the most diverse social and communal contexts between people without these all being rooted in destiny. These connections and contexts are not all prepared in advance in previous lives but instead in the period you pass through between death and a new birth, especially towards the second half of this life after death, when the prospect of a new birth arises. Then you enter into a relationship with beings, above all of the higher hierarchies, and are influenced by their powers in a way that melds you spiritually with diverse groups of human beings. The spiritual, cultural life you experience in the context of religion, art, nation, or even by virtue of sharing a common language, or through a very specific form of education and so on, is all prepared in pre-birth life but in a way that is distinct from purely karmic factors. At birth you bring with you into physical life on earth what you previously experienced in your pre-birth life. And these pre-birth experiences come to expression in cultural life, the life of spirit, in this earthly realm, albeit in a quite different way from how you experienced them before birth.

A very specific question will arise here for someone who is able to give all due seriousness to this kind of spiritual reality: how do we rightly serve this earthly culture of ours, in a higher sense, when we know that it is an earthly reflection of what we actually experienced in our spiritual existence before birth? We can only properly serve it if, instead of regarding it as ideology, we know that the world of spirit indwells it. We only develop the right stance towards this life of earthly culture if we are aware that the powers of the world of spirit are everywhere active within it. Take it as a hypothesis, if you like, that the thoughts of beings of spirit belonging to the super-sensible world—whether beings of the higher hierarchies who never assume an earthly body, or unborn human beings who have not yet entered upon their future life at birth—are alive, that their soul life lives in a kind of dream reflection within our earthly culture. And so it is quite legitimate for us to ask ourselves what lives in any artistic or religious or educational impulse that we encounter. We do not meet here something that humankind has simply created on earth but rather something that lives in it, streams into it from powers, thoughts, impulses, from the whole soul life of the higher hierarchies. We never see the world in its entirety if we deny that our earthly culture is informed by the reflected thoughts of spirit beings not embodied on the earth—who either are never embodied or are not so at present. If we can acquire a feeling of the sacred nature of the world of spirit, as the gift of spirit beings all around us who compose the spiritual world, then we can find a due sense of gratitude for these supersensible gifts which we experience as our earthly culture. And then this spirit-borne world of culture will inevitably find its proper and necessary place in humanity's whole social organism, as the furtherance of what we ourselves participate in before birth in the world of spirit. If we illumine the life of society through spiritual insight, it becomes self-evident that this cultural life of ours must have a distinct and autonomous reality.

The second sphere of society can be called the external legislative state, or political life in its narrower sense—everything that relates to legal relationships between people, in which all are equal before the law. This is the life of nationhood, of the state, which should comprise no more than this. Here again, certainly, our healthy common sense can show us the need for this state legislature, this life of public justice, which concerns the equality of all before the law, the equal rights of all human beings, to be an autonomous sphere of the social organism. And yet we can become aware of something quite different too in this domain if we study it with vision made keener by anthroposophic spiritual science.

This sphere of law and justice is the only domain in society which has nothing to do either with pre-birth or after-death existence. It is an order and orientation established only in the world in which we live between birth and death. Only to this degree is the state, archetypally, a self-contained whole, as long as it does not impinge on anything that in some way relates to the supersensible world, whether looking back to pre-birth life or forward to life after death. 'Render unto Caesar the things that are Caesar's and unto God the things that are God's.'[10] But we can make this still clearer by adding:

'Do not render unto Caesar the things that are God's, nor unto God the things that are Caesar's.' In both cases they will be repudiated!

We need to clearly and cleanly distinguish these things, in the same way that different systems in the natural human organism are kept separate. Everything which the state encompasses, which can be discussed and agreed at a legislative level, relates solely to the social coexistence of human beings. That is the important thing, and deeper religious sensibilities have invariably felt this throughout history. Others, not gifted with a deep religious nature, did not even allow people to discuss these matters freely and honestly, because of a conviction that took root in those of deeper religious sensibility. The latter knew that the state only encompasses the life between birth and death, all that concerns merely earthly existence. And it is a bad thing when earthly concerns seek to extend their reach and dominion to the supersensible realm, to what lies before birth and after death. Earthly human culture is something that originates beyond birth and death, for it contains shadows, reflections, of the soul experiences of supersensible beings. When impulses living in the life of rights and legislature sought to take over the life of spirituality on earth, of human culture, people of deeper religious sensibility saw this as a power exercised or usurped by the iniquitous prince of this world.[11] This phrase—'the iniquitous prince of this world'—relates to what I have now described. And this was also why the circles interested in confounding and confusing the three distinct spheres of the social organism do not like hearing it spoken, and frown upon this expression.

Something different, again, holds true in our thinking, feeling and inner impulses in so far as we are involved in the economic sphere of the social organism. There is something very curious and distinctive here, though by now, schooled as you are in anthroposophically oriented spiritual science, you will be used to grappling with seemingly paradoxical realities. When we speak of the economic sphere of the social organism, we have to be clear that in the terms we mean it now it is characteristic of the fifth post-Atlantean epoch only. In former ages of humanity's evolution these things were different.

What I have to say therefore relates to our life today and in future. In earlier times humankind engaged more instinctively in economic life, whereas now this must become ever more conscious. As I have said previously, in the same way that we learn our times tables in primary school, and other basic things, in future we will have to learn at school the things that relate to the social organism, to economic life. We have to be able to feel that we are a part of the economic organism. Naturally some will find this uncomfortable since they are used to other habits of thought and feeling, and these habits must change entirely. If someone today does not know what three times nine is, he will be considered uneducated. In some circles you will be thought uneducated if you do not know who Raphael or Leonardo was. But you are not generally regarded as uneducated if you are unable to define the nature of capital, production, consumption and the way these interrelate, or what the credit system and banking involves, and so on, not to mention the fact that very few people indeed have any clear idea of the meaning of a 'Lombard business' and suchlike.

As social conditions change these concepts will no doubt change too, and it will become easier in future to seek and find clarification of such matters. Nowadays people feel rather flummoxed if they try to fathom economics. Picking up a book on economics by an acknowledged expert in the field—for what could be more natural when trying to understand the subject?—you will be confused to find that different economists all give quite different definitions of capital. What would you think about the subject of geometry if you were to read three books about it and find that the theorem of Pythagoras is presented quite differently in each? Even acknowledged authorities on economics seem unable to clarify their subject, and one can therefore scarcely find fault with the general public for failing to seek more insight. But insight will be needed. People will have to build a bridge that connects them with the economic structures of the social organism. They will have to integrate themselves, their subjective existence, into economic life, into the social organism. They will have to learn to think about how they

relate to others in this realm simply by virtue of the fact that they
engage economically with others in a particular territory in relation
to all kinds of goods and commodities. The thinking we develop
here, informed by our whole relationship with the natural world, is
quite different in kind from, say, the thinking that develops in the
world of human culture. In this other realm, of spirit and culture, you
gain an experience of the thinking of beings of the higher hierarchies,
and of what you yourself experienced in your pre-birth life. In the
thinking you develop as a participant in the economic struggle for
survival, as paradoxical as this may seem, another person, a deeper
person, is always thinking alongside and within you. Specifically
when you feel yourself to be part of an economic entity, a deeper
person is thinking in you and alongside you. Here, with your
thinking, you are obliged to compile and conflate diverse factors of
outward life. What will the right price be for this or that? How do I
obtain one or another commodity? And so forth. Here your thoughts
in a sense flit from one outward fact to the next, and your thinking is
not informed by spirit but by outward, material things. And it is
precisely because outward material factors live in your thinking,
which has to be alert here to what is happening in economic life, and
not merely instinctual experience as in the animal, that we can say
that another, deeper human being is continually thinking within you
about these things. He is the one who perpetuates these thoughts,
creating connections between them and giving them a provisional
conclusion. And this deeper person within you is an essential participant in everything you carry with you into the world of spirit at
death. However paradoxical it may seem to many, consideration of
material factors we are obliged to engage in here in the world, which
are never finished and never come to a final conclusion, stimulates in
us another inner, spiritual life that we carry through death into the
supersensible world. Thus the feelings and impulses we develop in
economic life have a closer connection with our life after death than is
commonly realized. This may seem very strange and paradoxical; and
yet it is simply a more conscious version of what entered human
instincts from the world of spirit in atavistic eras of human evolution,

and developed in humankind back then. Let me clarify this with the following thoughts.

In certain indigenous tribes you can discover very striking social arrangements. Now we must not entertain the nonsensical and foolish idea about such tribes that modern anthropologists propound. The latter think that these tribes, the Aborigines in Australia for instance, are a throwback to humanity's earliest stages, and that modern 'civilized' peoples once originated from such a state. This is nonsense! In fact these indigenous tribes represent an element that has lapsed from an earlier condition, becoming decadent. The only difference between these tribes and supposedly civilized peoples is that they have retained aspects of their earlier condition whereas in so-called civilized people this has been masked or overlaid. For this reason we can study in indigenous peoples much that once existed in humankind at times of atavistic clairvoyance, when, for example, the following social arrangements existed. The members of a particular tribe formed small groups, each of which had a certain name taken from a plant or animal of that region. This delineation of smaller groups within larger social contexts was connected with the following. One group, say—but here we will use modern names just to clarify what I mean—bore the name 'rye'; and this group had to ensure that rye was properly cultivated so that other groups (not called 'rye') could be supplied with the grain. Thus these people had to supervise rye cultivation and distribution, while other groups, with different names, could depend on supplies of rye from them. Another group might be called 'cattle', and had the task of husbanding cows, supplying produce from them to the other groups. Besides supplying the product for which they were responsible, as designated by their names, at the same time it was forbidden for other groups to cultivate a product not assigned to them. This was the 'totemic right', as it was called, of each group. This is the economic meaning of 'totem', which was at the same time part and parcel of a mystery culture in the regions where these totemic practices existed. Mystery culture was not, as modern people imagine, something altogether lofty and removed from daily life, but, drawn from the resolves of the gods which participants in the mysteries could decipher, it played into the smallest everyday details of existence as a socially organizing influence. It ordered the tribe according to totemic forms, totemic groups, and thus brought about a corresponding economic order. At the same time, in specific ways, it disclosed to people the intrinsic nature of the world of spirit, showing how this world enters into and informs earthly culture, in a way that was appropriate at the time. As well as governance through the life of rights, with its solely earthly character, people here on earth prepared themselves through their economic arrangements and institutions so that at death they could once again enter a world in which they must develop connections that they could only previously prepare on earth through their engagement with the non-human realms of nature. These ancient tribes learned, through the guidance of their initiates, to include in their life on earth a sphere of economics with its due relationship to the cosmos.

Later this grew less and less clearly distinguished, although it is not too difficult to trace an instinctive threefolding of the social organism up to ancient Greece and even into medieval culture, and, in its vestiges, discernible up to the eighteenth century. Ah, modern people think in such superficial ways—they prefer things to be presented so easily and comfortably. A deeper study of former times, rather than commonly accepted legends that nowadays make up much of what is thought to be history, will show that threefolding was practised instinctively, and that in one sphere of the social organism, that of spiritual life, everything originated from a spiritual centre and was thus separate and distinct from state governance.

When the Catholic Church was at its height, it created an autonomous sphere which in turn organized the rest of earthly culture as an autonomous domain, founding schools, organizing education, including the first universities. It made earthly culture autonomous, ensuring that the state was not pervaded by the iniquitous prince of this world. And in economic life, even in later times, a sense at least prevailed of a fraternity between people as a preparation for something that will be perpetuated in the life after death. The idea that brotherliness will be rewarded after death is in fact an egotistic reinterpretation of the higher insights that once lived in totemism, but shows at least some residual awareness that fraternal life in human economics will be perpetuated in a realm of spirit after death. Even perversions in this realm must be judged from the same perspective. They lie in human nature. The medieval sale of indulgences was one of the worst excesses and yet it too sprang from an awareness that the economic sacrifice a person makes here in physical life has significance for his life after death. Although a caricature of the truth, it was a caricature originating in a true perception of what we experience when we relate on earth to the natural realms of the minerals, plants and animals. By entering into relationship with other creatures we acquire something that only fully unfolds in life after death. As far as our after-death condition is concerned, you see, we are still related here to lower forms of life, to animals, plants and minerals, and precisely in this experience of non-human entities we prepare something that will only grow up into our human nature after death. Our experience of animals, plants and minerals is an encompassing element for us on earth, surrounding us like a spiritual atmosphere within the earthly realm, whereas what people experience amongst each other is the basis only for a purely etheric element between birth and death.

What we experience below the human level, in economic life, only becomes human as such, is only raised into an earthly human element, once we have crossed the threshold of death.

For someone with an anthroposophic orientation, who seeks to deepen his insights into life through anthroposophy, this ought to be of the very greatest interest: to acknowledge that this threefold social organism is tangibly founded in our own threefold being, and this because we bear something with us of what we experienced before birth as we grow into the physical world in childhood; and bear also in us something that only has meaning between birth and death, and, as it were, below the veil of ordinary physical life prepares something that will have meaning in our supersensible existence after death. What appears here as the lowest realm of life, you see, our life in the physical economy which seems of a lower order than the sphere of rights and justice, nevertheless compensates us by gaining time for us to prepare ourselves for life after death as we engage in 'lower' economic activity. In our soul's participation in art, religious life, education and other forms of culture, we consume the inheritance which we bring with us at birth into earthly, physical life. But by lowering ourselves in a sense below the human level through economic life, into a realm of thinking that does not raise itself so high, we are compensated by preparing in our deepest self something that only after death will raise itself to the human level. This may still sound paradoxical to modern ears since people nowadays see things so narrowly and reject any sense that everything in life has two aspects. Something lofty from one perspective is of a lower order from another. Everything in life really has two aspects, and we would gain better insights into ourselves and the world if we were aware of this. Sometimes it feels uncomfortable to entertain such a thought in its full scope for it imposes various duties on us. For instance, we have to practise a degree of cleverness in certain respects, but actually we cannot develop the necessary acuity without at the same time developing an equal measure of stupidity in another direction. The one always incurs the other. Really we ought never to think a person completely stupid, even if he appears so in outward life, without being aware that a deep though concealed wisdom may lie in his subconscious. Reality only comes into focus before us if we take full account of its dual aspect. The life of spirit and culture appears to us to be very lofty on the one hand; but at the same time it is the realm in which we are actually always practising theft, consuming what we bring into physical existence at birth. Economic life seems to us to be the lowest aspect of human activity but this is only because it reveals its lowest aspect here between birth and death. In fact it allows us the time to develop, unconsciously, the spiritual aspect of economic life, which we bear into supersensible realms at death. And what I mean, primarily, by the spiritual aspect of economic life is a sense of commonality and community with other human beings.

It is an urgent necessity that humanity should understand these things if it is to emerge from certain calamities arising precisely from the fact that no account has been taken of them. Amongst leading members of the ruling intelligentsia something has emerged—I spoke of this the day before yesterday[12]—which does not have sufficient impetus to enter daily life. It is particularly important for us today to acquire the right understanding of this. You see, the ruling intellectual classes of society have developed a certain moral world-view, a certain religious outlook. Yet this is a moral, religious outlook that they prefer to cultivate in a narrowly idealistic manner, and which therefore does not gain the momentum to enter ordinary daily life. Attending church Sunday after Sunday, and perhaps more frequently, you will hear sermons which continually avoid grappling with the most pressing tasks of our day. You will hear all kinds of things you are urged to do in accordance with a religious world-view, but it has no purchase on reality. Then, leaving the church, and once more entering daily life, you find it impossible to put into practice these sermons about love between human beings, about how you should live your life. How can you forge a connection between what the preacher or moral instructor says to his flock and the conditions actually prevailing in daily life?

Things were different in this respect in the days when the totemic rites held sway; in those times the initiates arranged life in accordance with the counsel of the gods. An unhealthy state of affairs existing today comes to expression in the fact that sermons in church say nothing about economic life and how it should be organized. What is preached from the pulpit—I have often used this simile—is like looking at a stove and saying to it: 'Stove, you stand here in the room. In your position relative to the other objects in this room it is your sacred duty to heat the room. Fulfil this sacred duty therefore, and make the room warm.' You can stand there preaching to the stove as long as you like, but the room will stay cold! Instead of preaching, you will be better advised to fetch wood or coal, place it in the stove and light it. Then the room will warm up. In other words, it would be better to leave aside all moral sermons to people to behave in ways that will bring them eternal bliss or suchlike, which simply appeal to their faith. Sermons are not essential, but what is essential is to cultivate real insight into the social organism. That would be the proper task of all who wish to instruct the populace: to build a bridge, also quite practically, from the living spirit which infuses everything to what actually happens in daily life. You see, God, the divine, does not only live in what people dream in rarefied heights but also in the tiniest detail of the everyday. The divine is present when you pick up the salt cellar from the table, when you bring a spoonful of soup to your mouth, when you buy something from someone else for five pence. You contradict the inmost significance of a world-view which truly accords with reality if you regard one aspect of life as merely material, tangible and lower in nature, and the other as divine spirit that must be kept nice and separate from this material and tangible realm—when you see the one as sacred and the other as profane. What we need instead is to find the impetus that draws the highest and most sacred down into the most ordinary, everyday human experiences.

Religion has developed in a way that fails to do this. It preaches to the stove to get hot but avoids engaging in real, tangible spirit knowledge. It would be very beneficial if people were to express this, state it clearly: that those who feel called upon to instruct others in spiritual matters actually fail to connect one realm with the other. Stating this would show the direction we need to go in.

How do people talk nowadays about redemption, grace, and all the articles of faith? They do so in a very easy and comfortable way: here we have people with their human sensibilities. Once upon a time Christ Jesus died at Golgotha and—though progressive theologians no longer believe this—was resurrected. But he did or does this all by himself and people need do no more than believe in it. That's the view of many nowadays, and they regard it as an annoyance if anyone thinks differently. But we have to learn to think differently! A radical renewal is needed specifically in this domain.

We can put it like this. The admonishment of Christ, or also already of John the Baptist, is once again resonant for us today: 'Change your ways, for the time of crisis is near at hand.'[13] People have become used to somehow assuming the spirit exists in some realm where it takes care of them, to relying on preachers who tell of the existence of a world of spirit but fail to describe it in any real way. People do not wish to exert their thinking enough to gain knowledge of the world of spirit, but are happy simply to believe in it. But the time has passed when this may be! A time must begin now when people have to know and not just believe things. Not just, 'I think, and maybe I also think about the supersensible occasionally,' but, 'I must allow divine-spiritual powers to enter my thinking and feeling. The world of spirit must live in me. My thoughts themselves must be divine in nature. I must give God an opportunity to express himself through me.' Then the life of spirit and culture will not remain mere ideology. That is the great sin of modern times, that culture and spirit have been diluted, weakened into ideology. Theology itself, and not just socialism, is now ideological. But people must recover from this ideology, so that the spiritual world becomes reality for them. They need to know that the world of spirit lives as reality in one sphere of the social organism as the legacy of pre-birth life, the world of spirit, and that another aspect of spirit is in preparation as we seemingly descend to lower realms and interact with other human beings in economic life. In this realm specifically, something is being prepared as balance to this submergence which, when we enter the world of spirit again at death will lead us in turn—if we fully and properly experience it—to more humane and fraternal knowledge here on earth.

We need to start seeing life's reality again. We place ourselves into the world in the right way as anthroposophists if we realize that things humanity need today can be deepened by developing spiritual science not just as theory but as something that penetrates all our feelings, pervading and transforming our whole sense of life, rendering it worthy to participate in what must now begin in our times and what alone will create wellsprings for humanity's future.

What has been omitted, and what is needed—only by engaging fearlessly and courageously with things that have been omitted and what is needed can anything healing for the present and near future come about. It is for this reason that I have tried here, in this more intimate circle, to add anthroposophic perspectives of a deeper kind to what one can say in public about the social problem, including here aspects of the immortal, supersensible life of disembodied human souls in their interaction with earthly life.

Only one sphere of the social organism, relating to the state's outward organization, is purely earthly. The two other spheres are quickened by two aspects of super-terrestrial reality. On the one hand we have an earthly cultural life with which we are endowed as a superfluity, garnered in a sense from a pre-birth, super-terrestrial life of spirit. And on the other hand, as corporeal human beings—and as such connected with the other creatures of the earth—we must submerge ourselves in merely economic activity. But we are not only corporeal. Within this body of ours, the soul is being prepared for subsequent lives on earth and subsequent supersensible life. In economic life something is being prepared that will raise a part of us that is not yet wholly human—the part of us that must be embedded in economic life—into the domain of the human. Within us, in a sense, we bear a partly superhuman aspect in so far as we can move towards a social context that is interwoven with earthly culture, with spirit on earth. We bear something merely human in us as citizens of the state. And we bear in us something that compels us to descend below both these, which the world of spirit at the same time compensates us for however, by preparing within this apparently lowest sphere of social experience something that will in turn lead us back and reintegrate us with the supersensible.

Reality is not superficial enough to be easily comprehended, even though many would prefer it to be so. Human life passes through the most diverse phases, and at each phase new momentum, new ingredients, new impulses enter life that can only emerge in the particular realms where they are given. We can observe how the threads of life which we spin here between birth and death are interwoven with the threads spun in the life between death and rebirth. Everything is meaningfully interwoven in this totality of human life. The threads spun between one human individual and another here in earthly life—what we do to someone by giving him pleasure, by inflicting an injury on him, by enriching his thoughts or impoverishing them, by teaching him something or other—prepares our karmic destiny in a subsequent life on earth.

But we must distinguish this from what we need in order to prepare ourselves for supersensible existence immediately after death. Here on earth we are led into certain social communities, from which we must be led forth once more. We are led forth from them by virtue of the fact that something surfaces from our merely economic activities, from mere economics, that guides us through the portal of death into the world of spirit so that we do not remain in the social community we found our way into here, but can depart from it and be received into another in our next life. In this very meaningful way the karmic weft connecting us here is interwoven with the warp of our more general life in the cosmos.

Insights we can gain from spiritual science about the ways in which supersensible life is connected with physical life on earth inform our understanding of the threefold social organism, substantially deepening the more exoteric content of this view. Naturally this is hard for others outside anthroposophy to comprehend, and there's nothing to be done about that. But within the anthroposophic movement we should look beyond earthly considerations and reasoning to encompass, at the same time, all that connects us with the sphere we enter at death, from which we came at birth, and in which we must seek those with whom we have certain connections who have passed before us from this earthly world. Deepening our insights into life through anthroposophy will lead to this finest of human achievements: an understanding of the two great mysteries of earthly life, birth and death, and the building of a bridge between sensory and supersensible reality, between the so-called living and the so-called dead. Then the dead can live amongst us, and we can see that life in the supersensible realm, which was ours before birth and will be ours again after death, is nothing other than a different form of existence. This existence is 'dead' as far as sensory reality is concerned, just as sensory reality is 'dead' while we live in the supersensible realm. Everything in the world is related and inter-woven. And only when we understand these two aspects of every reality can we fully fathom it.

I wanted to offer these thoughts today to enlarge on more esoteric aspects of issues we so urgently need to discuss in public. It is very important that people close to the anthroposophic movement should participate in these public debates.

In reply to a question that was not recorded, Rudolf Steiner added:

This view of the social organism is, one can really say, a firm foundation. We simply have to study how it can be integrated with reality in each specific instance.

If you know Pythagoras' theorem, you will not ask how it is justified in every single instance. When you know it, then you also know it holds true wherever it is applicable, just as 3 times 10 is always 30 however you apply this knowledge. There will be no need to ask if it is correct in principle, nor will you have to keep proving it. You just have to recognize the truth of it yourself. In the same way, in relation to this view of society, we start from a certain firm foundation that is simply true, and other things will follow and relate to this primary insight in the right way. The tax system, the capital ownership system—everything will accord with this primary insight. All this will become clear if we comprehend the nature of the living social organism. And so, for instance, people will not hold back from sending their children to the Free Waldorf School. On the contrary, they will *want* to send them; they will have an interest in doing so.

And likewise in the sphere where each person develops a relationship with every other, the rights sphere, it is necessary to form correct judgements; and no one could be elected to join a representatives association of this second sphere of the social organism without this capacity for judgement. Naturally this has to be checked. But relationships between people, this active interest, this conscious involvement in life, is something that will certainly be self-sustaining in the free and ever healthier social organism.

LECTURE 3

As people interested in the anthroposophic movement, as I said a week ago, we are in a position to substantially deepen and more fully comprehend the burning social issues of today, and to recognize what humanity needs at present. We can find a proper view and stance towards these issues, one deeper than is possible in the broad public domain. If I may speak in biblical terms, we can see ourselves as a kind of leaven, with each person, wherever they live, contributing something especially needed at present out of their deeper feelings and impulses.

Recalling the basic tenor of the public lectures,[14] we see the need today to seek for a certain division and structuring of the social organism. The word 'seek' is important, indicative not of some kind of revolutionary programme we want to realize as soon as possible, but an effort to create a certain organized division of what has become centralized under various modern influences. Instead of the so-called centralized state, we wish, alongside other spheres of the social order, for a distinct and independent sphere to develop comprising everything that relates to spiritual life, to culture: education, teaching, art, literature, and also, as I have indicated, and will touch on tomorrow in the public lecture,[15] all that relates to the administration of civil and criminal law. A second sphere of the social organism should encompass more strictly what has so far been called 'the state' which in modern times, influenced by the preceding four centuries, has been invested with all kinds of diverse tasks: state education and so on. Under the influence also of socialist and social ideas, people seek nowadays to weld together economic life and what one can truly call the political life of rights into a single unity. Both need to pull apart again. As a second, autonomous sphere of the social organism, the political state must be distinct and separate from the third sphere, an independent, relatively independent economy, comprising the circulation of goods and commodities.

Today I would like to consider this subject from a perspective that will not be so easy to understand for someone not affiliated to our movement; I wish to bring it to a certain conclusion and culmination, from which can emerge a deeper understanding of the situation for modern humanity in general. Let us first consider what people call 'culture' in an earthly sense. This is everything that raises us in any way beyond our individual egoism as human beings, and gathers us into community with other people. Let us take the area of culture and spirit still of most significance for the majority of people today, one which aims to convey our connection with the life of spirit that is not of this world: religious life in other words, of whatever denomination or confession. Here we gather together with other people with whom we share similar needs of soul. Through education, too, one person cares for another in a soul-spiritual sense. When we read a book we are also led beyond our own immediate, individual, egoistic life. If the book becomes popular even to a limited degree, we then share the same thoughts with numerous other people who also read it, and this likewise places us in a certain group of people who experience something similar in their souls. This is an important characteristic of spiritual life, of culture, that it springs from complete freedom, from the individual initiative of each person, but that this earthly cultural life then leads us into community with others, giving rise to groups of people within the entirety of humanity.

But for someone who seeks deeper understanding, such commonality at the same time leads us closer to the key event of all earthly evolution, the Mystery of Golgotha. Since the Mystery of

Golgotha took place within the earth's evolution, everything that relates to human community in a sense also belongs to this Christ impulse. This is the thing of chief importance: that the Christ impulse does not belong to each separate individual but to human community. In accord with the nature of Christ Jesus himself, it is a great error to think that an individual, as such, can have a direct relationship with the Christ. Essentially, Christ lived, died and was resurrected for humanity in its entirety. And therefore since the Mystery of Golgotha, the Christ event, is—as we will return to later—always of immediate relevance whenever any kind of human community develops. If we really understand the world we find that earthly culture too, springing from the most individual aspect of us, from our personal potential and gifts, also relates to the Christ event.

But now let us consider this earthly culture of ours in its own terms: religious life, education and schooling, art and so on. Through this culture we enter into a certain relationship with others. And here we have to distinguish between what brings us into relation with other people through our own destiny, our karma, and what is not intrinsically or intimately connected with this karma. On the one hand we have certain relationships with people that arise in our life: we form new connections with certain people. We have relationships that are nothing other than the outcomes of other relationships we formed in previous lives on earth. And here in this life, in turn, we forge relationships that will give rise to karmic developments in succeeding lives. This produces a whole range of individual relationships with other people. Such connections, intrinsically related to our more intimate karma, must be distinguished from further relationships we enter into through commonality and community, for instance by virtue of our membership of a religious community, a faith community, or because we are educated in the same way, read the same books and so forth, enjoy the same works of art. These people with whom we are in community on earth are not invariably connected with us through relationships in former lives. There are however communities of people who are related to each other karmically, sharing a common destiny, but this is not usually the case with cultural and faith communities. But this leads us back to something else: to the end of the period which we pass in the supersensible world between death and rebirth. When we are close to the time of being reincarnated on earth, we enter into spiritual relationships—since by then we have become mature enough to do so—firstly with the hierarchies of the Angeloi, Archangeloi and Archai, with the higher hierarchies altogether; but we also come close to other human souls in the time preceding our rebirth, people who will have longer to wait than us before they are reborn. We have a whole range of supersensible encounters at this time, having become mature enough for them, before we are drawn back again into earthly life through birth. And these powers we absorb place us back on the earth in a location where it becomes possible for us to experience the kinds of earthly cultural communities I just described.

From what I have said it will be apparent, above all, that our earthly culture and life of spirit, which we experience as religious people, in our education and upbringing, in the impressions we receive from art and suchlike, is not dictated and determined merely by earthly things, but by what we previously experienced in supersensible realms before we descended through birth to this earthly culture. Just as a mirror image points us to a reflected reality, so earthly culture points us to what we experienced before we descended into our earthly body. In this respect, there is nothing so intrinsically and truly vividly connected with the super-sensible world as this earthly culture, despite the many aberrations apparent in it. In fact even these aberrations have a meaningful connection to what we experience, albeit in a quite different way, in the supersensible realm. Earthly culture acquires a very distinctive place in the world because it is connected with our life before birth. Nothing else in our earthly life is so closely connected with our pre-birth life as this earthly culture. A spiritual researcher must point this out clearly. He distinguishes earthly culture from other human activities which people on earth are involved in because his supersensible observations show him that this earthly culture has its origins, its impulses in supersensible life before birth, and in this respect it is different in quality from other human experiences.

What we can identify in stricter terms as political life, public legislature and rights, the state which establishes order amongst humankind, is different in kind. One can apply the most precise spiritual-scientific methodology in studying what this state as such, the political life of rights, has in common with anything else, but no connection will be found between this and a supersensible realm. This sphere is entirely earthly, although we must carefully clarify what is meant by this. What exactly is an earthly legal relationship? It is a relationship of property or ownership. If I own a piece of land, say, I only do so because a political context gives me the exclusive right to make use of it, enabling me to exclude all others from its use or cultivation. Everything based on public law is the same. The sum of all civil laws, and also the sum of everything which a particular community defends as its rights or property, amounts to the life of the state in its narrower sense. This is earthly life *per se*, and is connected only with the impulses active in us between birth and death. However much the state may sometimes consider itself to have God-given rights, a deeper view of all religious confessions will show us the following: firstly, what Christ Jesus meant when he said, 'Render unto Caesar what is Caesar's, and unto God what is God's.' By saying this he sought to counter the aspirations of the Roman Empire by showing that the external life of the state is distinct from all that is a reflection of supersensible life. But everything that seeks to introduce a supersensible impulse into the merely earthly life of the state, for instance trying to make the state responsible for religious life or education—the latter, sadly, now regarded everywhere as the right approach—was regarded by deeper religious sensibilities in the past as an invitation to the iniquitous prince of this world to hold sway. This, they said, will be the result of merging spiritual, supersensible concerns with the external state.

What is meant by the 'iniquitous prince of this world' is not something you will fathom without the aid of spiritual science. This prince holds sway whenever what should govern only earthly circumstances aspires to incorporate spiritual, cultural concerns and, as we will see, also economic life. The prince entitled to hold sway in the world is the one who aspires only to encompass political relationships in their stricter sense: all that relates to and draws its impulses from our life between birth and death alone. Thus we have understood the second sphere of the social organism in terms of spiritual science: it is oriented only to the impulses active in us between birth and death.

And now we come to the third sphere, that of economic relations. Picture the fact that economic life places us really into a certain relationship with the world. You will easily come to see the nature of this relationship if you imagine how it might be possible for us to become entirely and exclusively absorbed in it. What would we be if our whole being and all our activity was involved in nothing but outward economic life? We would be nothing more than thinking animals. We only avoid becoming thinking animals by virtue of the rights life that we also engage in: a political life, the life of the state; and also a life of the mind, an earthly culture and spiritual life. Through economic life we are more or less pushed downwards below the human level, but as this occurs, in this sphere specifically, we can develop interests that are most eminently fraternal. In no other sphere can we so easily and self-evidently develop fraternal relations with others in the fullest sense of the word as in economic life.

What really holds sway in cultural, spiritual life on earth? Basically it is personal interest: inner preoccupation of an egoistic nature. People wish religion to save or bless them, or make them happy. Education exists to develop a person's particular potential. We enjoy art or practising art and look to it to enhance our life or bring joy to it, or also to nurture our life forces. It is invariably so that egoism, of a subtler or grosser kind, leads us, for our own sake, to earthly culture. This is quite understandable.

In rights life, political life as such, we have something that makes us equal before the law. Here we are concerned with inter-personal relations and the ways they are governed. We are concerned with our rights. Rights do not exist between animals, and this is something that elevates us over them already here in earthly life. In the circumstances obtaining in a religious community, an educational community, and also in a legislative community, we have something that in a sense is based on something to which we lay claim in a self-evident manner. But in the sphere of economic life, precisely if we can overcome our own perspective, something can emerge that is not founded on our own interests and volition: fraternity, consideration of the other; a way of living that enables the other to experience something through and alongside us.

In a spiritual relationship we receive something because we wish it. In a legal or rights relationship we lay claim to something if we wish, as we inevitably do, to maintain a dignified life as one among equals. And in economic life there unfolds something—fraternity—that connects the feelings of one person with those of another. The impulses of fraternal life arise when we create a certain relationship that bridges between what we possess and what the other possesses, and between what we need and the other needs, and so forth. When we increasingly develop this fraternity in economic life, then something else emerges from it. This fraternity in economic life, this fraternal relationship between people which must illumine economic life if it is to become wholesome and healthy, in a sense rises from it like vapour so that, having developed this fraternity in economic life, educated ourselves to do so, we take it with us through the gate of death and bear it on with us into supersensible life after death.

In our earthly perception, economic life seems to be the lowest form of human activity, but within it there develops something that pulses forth from earthly life, passing through the gateway of death into the supersensible. Thus we have considered the third sphere of the social organism in spiritual-scientific terms. It develops something that pushes us down into a subhuman realm in a sense, but we are compensated for this by the fact that we take the fraternity we develop in economic life with us through the gate of death—it stays with us when we enter the world of spirit. Just as earthly culture, the life of the mind, develops as I described earlier as a mirror image of pre-birth supersensible existence, so economic life, with the social interest, feelings of human community and fraternity it develops in us, points us forward towards supersensible life after death.

Here therefore we have distinguished three separate spheres: spiritual, cultural life, pointing back to pre-birth supersensible life; the state in its strict sense, related to impulses that unfold between birth and death; and economic life that points us towards what we will experience after we have passed through the gate of death. The human being is not just an earthly being but also, at the same time, a super-earthly one: he bears in him the fruits of what he experienced in his life before birth in the supersensible realm; and he develops the seeds of what he will experience in his life after death. Human life is threefold, and alongside these two forms of reflection of supersensible life there is a third realm we experience between birth and death that is specifically of the earth. Just as our life itself is threefold, so the social organism in which we live must be threefold in nature if the human soul in its entirety is to find its firm and stable foundation within this social organism. If we recognize our place in the cosmos through spiritual science, we discover far deeper reasons for acknowledging that the social organism has to be threefold. We can discern that human beings will degenerate—and in fact have done so in a sense in modern times, leading to the terrible catastrophe of the last four years[16]—if everything is centralized, and everything in the outward life of society is informed by chaotic, anarchic dis-organization. Gradually, through anthroposophic deepening of our insights, we should come to recognize the nature of human life and grow aware that the entirety of human nature must find its place within humanity and the world as a whole in the way I have described. At the same time this embodies the right form of Christ knowledge in our day and the near future. This is what is revealed to us if we wish to hearken to the Christ. He himself said, as I have often reiterated, 'I am with you always, even unto the end of the world.'[17] This means that what he uttered was not spoken only in the times when he walked upon earth, but that he continues to speak to us, and we should continue to hearken to him. Besides reading the Gospels, which of course we always continue to do, we should try to attend to what his living presence amongst us can reveal. In the modern era he reveals to us, as his forerunner John the Baptist said,[18] that we should change our ways, and this will show us a vision of threefold humanity which also requires us to structure in threefold form the earthly conditions in which we live.

People rightly say that Christ died and was resurrected for all humanity, that the Mystery of Golgotha is an event concerning all mankind. We can become particularly aware of this today when nation has risen against nation, when they have devastated one another in dire conflict; and when now, after a culmination and crisis in this warfare, instead of pause for contemplation, instead of awareness of the whole human community, a victorious delirium prevails. We must not overlook this. Everything we have experienced in the past four-and-a-half years, what we are now witnessing, and what will still come, shows those of deeper discernment that humanity has entered a crisis state as far as its awareness of Christ is concerned. And this is because people have lost sight of a proper sense of community, the right sense of connection with each other. It is essential that they start asking how they can rediscover the Christ impulse once more.

A simple fact can show us that many are failing to find it. Before the Christ impulse began to work into earth evolution through the Mystery of Golgotha, the nation into which Christ Jesus was born considered itself the 'chosen people', believing that the earth could only prosper if all else dies away and only the members of this nation fill the whole world. In a sense this was a firm conviction and matter of faith: the God Yahweh had chosen this people as his own, and he was regarded as the one God. In the times prior to the Mystery of Golgotha this was a justified view amongst the ancient Hebrews because Christ Jesus was indeed to come forth from this people. But when the Mystery of Golgotha occurred on earth, this outlook should have come to an end. After the Mystery of Golgotha it was outdated, and Yahweh consciousness should have ceded to Christ consciousness, which speaks in the same way of all human beings as the people of Yahweh spoke of the members of only one people. It is the tragic fate of the Jewish people that it did not recognize this. But today in many quarters we are witnessing a lapse into such mindsets; gradually, even if they do not see it or name it in this way, nations are succumbing to a kind of Yahweh, one specific to their own race, whom they worship as their national idol.

While people do not speak in the same religious formulae as in the past, it is the same outlook couched in modern terms, a modern way of thinking. A way of thinking or habit of mind might be a good way to put it, though nowadays people use a different term. To gain better understanding of it one might make the concession of adopting this way of thinking for a while, and instead of using the term 'habit' or 'way' of thinking, which I have always used in our circles, to employ the word 'mentality' or 'mind-set'. In the modern mentality, therefore, every nation seeks to establish its own distinct national god and promote these national qualities. It is precisely this that has led to nation warring with nation: we find here a lapse into the Yahweh religion, although here it is splintered into many different Yahweh religions. What we're seeing today really is a lapse into Old Testament atavism. Humanity seeks to sunder itself into separate parts across the whole globe, at odds with Christ Jesus whose living being served all humanity. Mankind seeks to inhabit the diverse national divinities, in a Yahweh-like way. Before the Mystery of Golgotha this was justified but is now outmoded, a lapse into an Old Testament condition. This lapse into the Old Testament mentality will bring with it severe trials for modern humanity, and there is only one remedy for this: to approach the Christ again upon a spiritual path.

This gives rise to a very particular question for those interested in spiritual science. In our day, how do we find our way to Christ Jesus out of the inmost impulse of our modern souls? That this is a very serious question—I have often spoken of it in this branch from other perspectives[19]—you can see from the fact that many official adherents of Christianity have really lost sight of the Christ. Nowadays there are many well-known priests, pastors and so forth who speak about the Christ, saying that human beings can gain a connection with him through a certain inner deepening of their sensibility. But if we look more carefully at what these people mean by Christ, one finds there is no difference between this and God in general, what is called God the Father, in the Gospels too. Harnack[20] is a theologian of repute, for instance, and here in Switzerland many look up to him. Harnack has published a little book, *The Nature of Christianity*, in which he speaks a great deal of Christ. But it is not at all clear that what he says of Christ has any particular relationship with Christ. Actually there is no reason to relate what he says to Christ at all, since it relates equally to the God Yahweh. For this reason the whole of *The Nature of Christianity* is inwardly untruthful. It only becomes true if we couch it back in the Hebrew tradition by removing references to Christ and replacing them instead by the word 'Yahweh'. This is a truth of which people today have scarcely any inkling. Sermons about Christ resound from countless pulpits round the world, and people believe that these sermons are authentic, that the name of Christ is truly spoken, simply because they hear the word 'Christ'. No one stops to ask whether, if one removed references to Christ from a priest's sermon and replaced it with 'Yahweh' it might not do just as well. In fact, only then will it read correctly! You see, there is a certain untruth connected with the profoundest flaws in our time. Please do not think that I wish to criticize anyone here or cast blame. This is not so. I wish only to express a fact. Those embroiled in the profoundest inner untruth, or inner lie one can say, do not know this and are certainly people of good will in their own way. Nowadays humanity finds it difficult to approach the truth because of the powerful obduracy with which tradition has established itself. And this inner untruth in respect of such things, which today spreads far and wide, gives rise to that other untruth which today has seized hold of the most diverse domains of life, so that it is hard to see any truth at all remaining. One has to ask where any truth or reality is still to be found. For someone who seeks spiritual-scientific insights, the question of how we can find the true path to Christ—to this distinctive divine being to whom the name of Christ rightly belongs—is therefore a very serious one. If our life is merely confined to the span between birth and death on earth, and a soul life that develops in accordance with our capacities and disposition in this realm, then we have no cause to come to Christ, however much goes on in our minds or spirit. If we do not do particular things, which I will describe in a moment, and simply develop between birth and death as most people do today, then we remain far from the Christ. But how can we approach the Christ? The initiative, even if this sometimes surfaces from the subconscious or an obscure feeling, to seek the path to Christ, to embark on this path, has to come from ourselves. We can find the God who is identical with the Yahweh God simply by living in an ordinary, healthy way. Not finding Yahweh is merely a kind of human illness. Denying God, being an atheist, means in a sense that one is ill. If we develop in any sense in a fully normal way, we will not be atheists since it is ridiculous to believe that the healthy organism we bear could not be divine in origin. The *ex deo nascimur* is something that arises by itself in the social existence of a person who develops healthily. You see, if he does not acknowledge that he is born out of God, he inevitably has a certain defect which comes to expression in his atheism. But this self-evident sense of being born out of God leads us only to the divine in general, which modern pastors, out of an inner lie, call Christ. It is not Christ. We only approach Christ—and I am speaking here of our immediate present—if we go further than simply acknowledging ordinary, God-given natural health. You see, we know that the Mystery of Golgotha occurred upon the earth because without it, without the Christ impulse, humankind could not have found its way into a truly human life, a life of human dignity. In a sense we can say that it is not enough to find our human nature between birth and death but we must also rediscover it if we wish to be Christians in the true sense, if we wish to come close to Christ. We have to rediscover this, our human nature, in the following way. We must seek, must exert ourselves to find, the inner honesty to say to ourselves: since the Mystery of Golgotha we are not born without prejudices in respect of our thought world. We are all born with certain biases or prejudices.

As soon as we regard the human being as inherently perfect, as

Rousseau does for example,[21] we cannot find the Christ. We can only find him if we know that as human beings living after the Mystery of Golgotha we have a flaw which we must remedy or compensate for in what we do in our life here. I am born as a person with prejudices, and have to gradually free myself from these in my thinking. How can I do so? Only by developing interest not only in what I myself think and what I consider right, but also selfless interest in everything human beings can think, all that approaches me however mistaken I consider it. The more a person insists that his own outlook and opinion is the only right one, and is only interested in this, the more he sunders himself from the whole world's evolution, from Christ. The more a person develops social interest in the views of others, even if he thinks them wrong or misguided, the more he will feel in his inmost soul the truth of a saying of Christ, which today must be interpreted in accordance with the new Christ language: 'Verily I say unto you, inasmuch as ye have done it unto one of the least of these my brethren, ye have done it unto me.'[22] Christ never ceases to reveal himself ever and again to human beings, until the end of all earthly days. He says this to those who wish to hearken to him: 'What one of the least of your brethren think, you must regard as me thinking in him; and I feel with you as you measure the other's thoughts against your thoughts, having social interest in what unfolds in the other's soul. Whatever you find as opinion, as outlook on life in one of the least of your brothers, seek therein for me.' It is thus that Christ speaks into our life of thought, seeking to reveal himself in a new way—we are approaching this time—to the people of the twentieth century. This is not Harnack's God, who might equally well be the Yahweh God, and actually is. Christ is, by contrast, the God of all humanity. We do not find him if we remain egotistically within our own thoughts, but only by measuring our own thoughts against those of others, enlarging our interest in inner tolerance for all that is human, saying to ourselves that we are born with prejudices but can be reborn out of the thoughts of all human beings into an encompassing social thought sensibility. Then we can find in ourselves the Christ impulse. If I do not regard myself alone as the source of all I think, but, right into my inmost soul, as a part of humanity, then I have found the path to Christ. This must today be called the thinking path to Christ. We can develop and educate ourselves in vital ways by acquiring a sense for the importance of how others think, thereby correcting the outlook we bear intrinsically within us through dialogue with others. This has to become a serious life task. If this task were not to make headway amongst humankind, people would lose the modern path to Christ which passes through thoughts and thinking.

The other path passes through the will. Here too people have embarked in a very misguided direction that does not lead to Christ but away from him. In this other realm too we must find the path to Christ. Youth still has its own natural idealism but in general humanity today has grown dry and prosaic. It is proud of what is often called 'pragmatism' although this is only practical in a certain narrow sense. Modern humanity looks very askance at ideals drawn from a source in the spirit. Youth still retains its ideals. Never before in history has the life of older generations been at such variance with that of the younger. A salient characteristic of our time is a failure to understand human nature.

Yesterday I spoke of the deep gulf that divides the proletariat from the middle classes.[23] But the older and the younger generation are similarly divided, and scarcely understand each other. We should pay very great attention to this. Let us try to understand the idealism of youth. Fine, you may say; but in fact great efforts are made nowadays to quash this idealism, and this is done by depriving young people of an education that addresses their imagination through fairy tales, legends, through all that leads them away from arid, external sensory facts and realities. Actually it is very hard to successfully quash this natural, youthful, elemental idealism. It is a lovely, vital quality, and yet cannot be the only human attribute since really this idealism emerges from the *ex deo nascimur*, from the divine ground of being that is identical with the Yahweh God. This must be complemented and enlarged ever since the Mystery of Golgotha took place on the earth. Alongside it there must be something else too: an education, a self-education for idealism. Alongside the innate idealism of youth we have to ensure that an acquired, self-developed idealism emerges in human communities—not just the idealism of young blood and enthusiasm but something we acquire by some kind of initiative. This is self-instilled idealism which is not lost as we age, and which opens the way to Christ because it is something that has to be acquired through our endeavours between birth and death. Try to sense the great difference between idealism of the blood and acquired, self-instilled idealism, the great difference between the fire of youth and the fire that comes from taking hold of the life of spirit and can be continually rekindled because we have developed it within us, independently of our bodily development. This is the second idealism, the acquired or reborn idealism rather than the one inherent in us. This is the path of the will to Christ, while the other is the path of thought. Do not seek abstract paths to Christ but seek these tangible ones: the path of thought through which we become inwardly tolerant of the views and outlooks of all humanity, gaining social interest in the thoughts of other people; and the path of the will that I have described—nothing abstract but acquiring, developing idealism. In developing this idealism, or instilling it in young people as they grow, which is especially necessary, you will find that people thereby develop a sense for doing not just what the outer world impels them to. Out of this idealism spring the impulses to do more than the sensory world impels them to, to act out of the spirit. In what we do in acquired, self-developed idealism we realize what Christ wished: he did not descend to earth from non-earthly realms to fulfil merely earthly aims but to realize super-earthly ones. But we only grow one with him if we cultivate idealism in ourselves so that Christ, who is super-earthly within the earth, can work in us. Only in this reborn idealism is realized the intent of the Pauline phrase 'Not I but Christ in me'.[24] If we do not seek to acquire self-developed idealism as our inner, moral rebirth, all that we can say is, 'Not I, but Yahweh in me.' But if we develop the idealism we must acquire and nurture, then we can indeed say, 'Not I but Christ in me.' These two paths I have described are the way to truly find the Christ and, pursuing them, our speech will no longer be inwardly untruthful. Then we will speak of the Christ as the God of our inner rebirth as opposed to Yahweh who is the God of our merely physical birth.

This difference and distinction is one we must discover today for this alone is what will lead us to truly social feelings, real social interest in others. Developing acquired idealism in ourselves we will also find love for others. You can sermonize as much as you like about loving your fellow human beings, but it is doing no more than telling the stove to heat itself. However nicely you speak to it, it will not get hot unless you put coal or wood in it. Then there will be no need to impress upon it its duty to warm the room. Preaching about love, love and more love is mere words. But working to help people experience a rebirth of idealism that sustains them in life, you are kindling neighbourly love too in the human soul. As you develop idealism within you yourself, your soul will lead you forth from egoism into self-reliant interest and feeling for others. However, one thing you will find as you pursue this twofold path of thought and will I have described in relation to the renewal of Christianity is an enhanced sense of responsibility towards everything we think and do, arising both from thoughts that are inwardly tolerant and interested in the thoughts of others, and from the reborn will emerging through self-developed idealism. Someone concerned to develop inwardly will, if he pursues both these paths, feel an enhanced, refined inner sense of responsibility towards all that he thinks and does, and this will be different in quality from the ordinary sense of responsibility of someone who does not pursue these paths. Can we discern an inner sense of responsibility which asks us whether we can justify a thought or action not just in regard to those closest to us, our immediate environment, but also in terms of our connection with a supersensible world of spirit? Can I justify something, knowing that everything I do here on earth is inscribed in an Akashic Record of eternal significance, where it goes on taking effect. Ah, how strongly you feel this supersensible responsibility towards everything. Like a being who stands behind you and looks over your shoulder, it approaches and admonishes you if you seek the twofold path of Christ. It continually tells you that you are responsible for all that you think and do, not just as regards the world but in relation to the divine, spiritual realm.

This being who looks over our shoulder, enhancing and refining our feelings of responsibility, and making them quite different in nature from what they used to be, is what leads us very close to the Christ who passed through the Mystery of Golgotha. I wanted to speak today about this path to Christ, about how it can be found and how it becomes apparent in the being I have just characterized. You see, this Christ path is intimately connected with the deepest social impulses and tasks of our time, and I wished to impress this on you in our gathering today.

Lecture 4

Zurich, 9 March 1919

THE way in which certain people feel prompted to speak about the current situation of humanity is really very significant. In a feeling way, at least, they try to grasp the nature of our social circumstances. To illustrate this, I would like to start our reflections today with some sentences from a talk which Kurt Eisner[25] gave to a group of students in Basel shortly before his death. Some of you may have heard these words already, but they are highly significant for a symptomatic evaluation of certain phenomena today. Picking up on things said previously, his words were as follows:

> Am I deaf to these things, or do I in fact see clearly that a longing is deeply rooted in our life and seeks air and light, recognizing that the kind of life we have to live today is clearly only the invention of some evil spirit? If you imagine a great philosopher who knew nothing of our age and lived around two thousand years ago, say, dreaming what the world would look like in two millennia's time, he would never in his wildest fantasies have conceived of the world in which we are condemned to live. The conditions that exist at present are the real illusion, and what lives as longing in us is the profoundest, ultimate reality. Everything else is horrendous. We are confusing dreaming and waking, that is all. Our task must be to shake off this old dream of our current social existence. If we

take a look at the war, we have to ask whether human reason could conceive of such a thing. If this war has not been what people call 'real', perhaps we have dreamed it all, and are now awakening again.[26]

So you see, in order to try to understand our present condition, this man resorted to the idea of dreaming. He poses the question whether the reality that now encompasses us can be seen as anything other than a bad dream rather than reality.

Let us reflect on this strange yet highly characteristic instance, in which a very modern human being, a mind at the forefront of things and someone who feels himself to herald a new age, is compelled by particular events of our day to describe not the whole of outward sensory reality as maya, an illusory dream, as say the ancient Indians regarded it, but to ask whether this social reality of ours might in some way be a dream. From the whole context of Eisner's talk we can see that he was not playing with phrases, that he really meant something he felt when he asked whether our present reality can be anything other than the machinations of an evil spirit.

Alongside this let us set much of what passes through our souls as we undertake our anthroposophic endeavours, above all the fact that we try to see outward sensory reality not as the whole of reality but as something whose counterpart is found in the supersensible, through which alone sensory reality is rounded into a whole reality. This view of ours is of course only a small spark in the currents of thought of our day, which are largely pervaded by materialistic thinking. Now a man such as Kurt Eisner, who from his own perspective certainly gives no credence to this little spark of ours, at least in his physical awareness, reaches for a particular metaphor to describe modern realities: that of a dream. Our outer reality, he says, is a dream from which we should awaken. In respect of our current social reality, a man like this is compelled to resort to a sense that our common reality is like maya, illusion: that merely outward sensory reality is unreal.

Let us now try to deepen some of the things we have been pondering in recent weeks in relation to the social question, in particular looking at the fact that over recent centuries people have increasingly come to deny the reality of the supersensible world, the world of spirit, and in the widest circles in fact actively oppose and repudiate such an idea. You may of course object that there is still much talk of spiritual things from a certain quarter. The churches may not be imbued with the spirit but words that are meant to express it do, at least, resound from them. Today and yesterday evening we have heard the church bells ringing almost continuously, supposedly an expression of the life of spirit in the world. But alongside this we encounter something else: that whenever efforts are made in our day to hearken to the Christ, to hear what he is saying to our times, then it is precisely the adherents of old religious traditions who most fiercely oppose this, who will not receive the word of spirit. Really very few people indeed seek a true life of spirit today, not one based on faith in an old tradition but on direct, immediate manifestations of the spirit.

In the face of this, isn't it possible that humanity today might be compelled—not by an evil spirit but by a good universal spirit—to recognize once more the spiritual nature of existence through its suffering of these outward sensory realities? A modern mind experiences this reality as an illusory dream, and a great philosopher of two millennia ago could not have conceived what seems to have become the outward reality in which we live.

At any rate, the fact that a modern mind sees things in these terms invites us to form different views of reality than are current today. I am aware that a great number of our anthroposophic friends find some degree of difficulty in these ideas about 'true reality' to which I have attributed importance today. But we cannot encompass life today without having the good will to address such difficult ideas. How do people think today in certain fields? Take a crystal in your hand: that is a real object. Likewise if you pick a rose from a rose bush and hold it in your hand you will say this is a real object too. But are they both real in the same sense? Scientists in all the universities and institutes, in all laboratories and clinics, see the crystal and the rose that is picked from a rose bush as sharing one and the same reality. But there is, surely, a huge difference between them implicit in the fact that the crystal retains its form through long ages while the rose, having been picked, will lose its form after a relatively short time, will die. It does not have the same degree of 'reality' therefore as the crystal. And even the whole rose bush, if we pull it up out of the ground, does not have the same degree of reality it has when it is rooted in the earth. This suggests we ought to regard things in the world in a different way from the external mode employed today. We ought not to speak of the reality as such of the rose or the rose bush but at most of the reality of the whole earth in which it is embedded, and upon which it grows from this reality as hair does on our heads.

You see therefore that there can be things in outer, sensory reality which, when divorced from their source or foundation, cannot be called real in the true sense. In other words, we must penetrate the great illusions of outer reality to find its true realities. Modern scientists make such errors in relation to reality. But making such errors, and habituating oneself to them over many centuries as humanity has done, means that it is very difficult indeed to cultivate social thinking in accord with reality. The major difference between human life and the life of nature is that the latter allows things to die when they are no longer invested with their full reality—like the rose plucked from a rose bush. An outward appearance of reality can also possess an unreality, something that is a lie as such. Something that has no intrinsic reality can however be realized in the life of society as if it were reality. It may not die immediately but it will gradually become pain and torment to humanity, whereas our wholesome well-being will only arise from something whose full reality has been felt, conceived and implanted into the human social organism. It is not just a sin against the social order but a sin against truth itself when, for instance, our modern outlook still assumes that human labour—I have often said this here—can be a commodity. Yes, we can make it into this in outward supposed reality, but this supposed outward reality will become pain and suffering in the human social order, giving rise to convulsions and revolutions in society.

In brief, today humanity needs to reconfigure its habits of thought, no longer seeing as sole reality what comes to expression in apparent, outward forms within narrow limits, and seeing in fact that this can be illusion or untruth. This difference between truth and lies in life ought to inscribe itself very deeply in our modern sensibility. As more and more people become aware of this distinction, and awaken within them a feeling that they must seek the truth in life and not lies or distortions, the more healthy the social organism will become. But what is necessary for this to happen?

It is not a self-evident thing to discover the true or only seeming reality of an external object. Imagine an alien arriving here from a planet where conditions are different, so that he could never have made the distinction between a rose growing on a rose bush and a crystal. If you then placed both before him, the rose and the crystal, he might think they were both of one common reality, but would be very surprised to find that the rose fades so quickly while the crystal retains its form. On earth we can only discern the nature of things because we become acquainted with them over longer spans of time. Yet we cannot trace the truth or otherwise of everything we see in outward reality simply by observing it like this. We can do so with the rose but there are other things in life which require us to create a foundation before we can discern their reality. As far as human social coexistence is concerned, specifically, how do we create such a foundation?

I have characterized some aspects of this in the two preceding lectures here,[27] and today I want to add a little more to this. From my books you will be familiar with the accounts I give of the world of spirit, of the world we pass through between death and rebirth. In describing this life in the supersensible world of spirit, as you know, we must take into account the relationships that hold sway there between one soul and another. Here the human being is free of the body, and not subject to the physical laws of this earthly world that we experience between birth and death, and we can speak in this respect of the powers or forces playing between souls. You can read in *Theosophy* about the powers of sympathy and antipathy unfolding between death and rebirth, inner forces in the interplay between souls in the soul world. One soul will bring antipathy to bear in relation to another, but this is assuaged by the opposite power of sympathies. Here harmonies and disharmonies arise between the inmost impulses souls experience. And this interrelationship between the inmost experience of one soul and that of another constitutes the true condition of the supersensible world. What one soul can experience with another here in the physical world is only a reflection, a vestige if you like of this supersensible experience.

But this reflection is something, in turn, that we must properly judge. We can ask this: in terms of social coexistence, how does what we experience here between birth and death relate to life in the supersensible realm? We have often spoken of the necessary three-folding of society, and now we must turn our attention to the middle realm as I have often described it, the political state as such. People who have thought about the political state in our times have always attempted to discern what it actually is. But you see, modern people with their materialistic ideas have no proper foundation for their reflections. The picture is complicated by the fact that in line with the interests of the different strata of society, the different classes, all sorts of things have been coupled with the modern state and so one can no longer simply assume that this state is a reality rather than a kind of lie. In our times a gulf has opened between the view of the German philosopher Hegel[28] and that of Fritz Mauthner,[29] the philosopher and dictionary compiler. Hegel sees the state more or less as the realization of God on earth, whereas Mauthner says it is a necessary evil. It is an evil, in his view, albeit one we cannot dispense with, which is necessary for human coexistence. So here we have the opposing outlooks of two modern minds.

Since a great deal that used to be configured instinctively is now the subject of conscious reflection, all kinds of people have tried to formulate ideas about the nature of the state and what it should be. One finds the most varied nuances and divergences in their ideas. On the one hand are the pious proponents of the state-as-it-is, who do not wish to intervene in its workings, and yet seek to shape it in a way that will if possible not ruffle the feathers too much of people who do indeed have cause to complain. And then there are the others who want to radically reshape society so that it might develop into a form of existence which would satisfy human beings. But what we first have to ask is this: how can we gain a view of what the state actually is?

We only gain insight into the reality of the state, its possible reality, if we consider with an open mind the threads that can be spun between one person and the next within the state, and compare this with threads spun between one soul and another in supersensible life. You see, the relationship founded on the deep, inmost powers of the human soul, on sympathies and antipathies in supersensible life, contrasts with the very external, rights-based relationship between people in the life of the merely political state. Here one person encounters another in the most external framework of common rights. If you think this through carefully, you will see that the state is the very opposite of supersensible life. And this state is all the more perfect in nature the more it is the exact opposite of life in the spirit, and the less it aspires, wrongly, to introduce something of supersensible life into its structure. It should only encompass the most external aspect of rights relationships between people and the way they conduct themselves towards each other. Here all men are equal, that is, equal before the eyes of the outward law. This truth is one that can become an ever deeper conviction in us: that the state's perfection consists precisely in the fact that nothing in it is sought except what belongs to the life between birth and death and is part of our most external form of interaction.

But then we have to ask this: if the state reflects supersensible life only by virtue of being the opposite of the latter, how does this supersensible realm enter the rest of our sensory life? I did describe this to you recently from another perspective. But today I wish to add this: that certain residues remain of the antipathies that develop in the supersensible realm between death and rebirth, residual antipathies which we carry with us into physical existence at birth. These residues are counteracted in physical life by everything that comes to expression in the life of spirit, cultural life, the life of the mind. Here people are brought together in religious communities, or in other shared perspectives and outlooks. This is so that they can balance certain antipathies that remain as residue from pre-birth life. Our whole culture and life of the mind needs to be a distinct sphere in society because it is a reflection of our pre-birth life, because in a sense it places us out into the sensory world with the gift of creating a kind of remedy for these residual antipathies left over from our time in the supersensible world. This is why it is so terrible when people cause ruptures and create adversarial factions in cultural life instead of properly uniting there as they should. The residual antipathies left over in us from our spiritual life before birth lurk in the underdepths of the human soul and prevent the aspirations we ought to have from becoming reality: real spiritual harmony, true spiritual collaboration. Where this ought to happen, sects and factions develop instead. These partisan groups and sectarian divisions are the sign, the reflection, of remaining antipathies from which all spiritual life emerges, but for which it should here provide a remedy. We must regard spiritual and cultural life as something that has an intimate connection with our pre-birth life, an affinity with it one can say. We should therefore not succumb to the temptation to establish this spiritual life of culture in any other way than as a free, independent life outside the state. The latter ought not to reflect supersensible life but be a counter-image of it. And we only gain a true idea of what really belongs to the state and what really belongs to the spiritual life of culture if we complement our sensory life with supersensible life. Only together do these two realms give us true reality, whereas merely sensory existence is certainly a dream.

Economic life is again quite different in nature. Here one person works for the other. Usually he does this because by doing so he finds advantage or benefit for himself, as the other does. Economic life arises from human needs and involves satisfying them: we elaborate on the physical plane everything that can satisfy or meet natural, mundane human needs, or also subtler and yet largely instinctive needs of soul. Unconsciously there develops within economic life something that in turn works on beyond death. The labour which people perform for one another in response to the egoistic needs of economic life develops subterranean seeds for certain sympathies that must form in our souls in the life after death. Just as the spiritual life of culture is a kind of remedy to heal the residual antipathies we bring with us into physical existence from our life before birth, so what unfolds in the underdepths of economic life is pervaded by seeds of the sympathies we should develop after death. Here is a different perspective on the need for a threefold social organism as it relates to supersensible life. But we cannot gain this perspective without attempting to understand the world through spiritual science. Someone who gains the right foundations for this knowledge will increasingly and self-evidently lend his voice, too, to demands for a tripartite division of the social organism if it is to become healthy. The three spheres of society each have a quite different relationship to supersensible reality which, as we have said, only constitutes the whole of reality in interplay with sensory existence.

Yet in the last two hundred years, humankind has said nothing about these conditions of outward physical existence, unfolding in the spiritual life of culture, in the life of the state and in economic life. Instead, old traditions have simply been perpetuated without understanding. Humankind has become unaccustomed to pursuing the path into the realm of spirit in direct inner activity, seeking there the light which can illumine physical reality. But only then do we fully and properly grasp physical reality. Leading circles have set the tone for this unspiritual way of life. And this has given rise to the deep cleft between social classes which now underpins all life and is something we really must not overlook. I have often reminded you that before the events of July and August 1914 members of the ruling classes kept praising the latest achievements of what they called our civilization. They pointed to the way in which thoughts could now be conveyed with lightning speed over great distances by means of telegraph and telephone, and how other fabulous achievements of modern technology had advanced the life of society and civilization. And yet this culture, this civilization rested on foundations that led to the terrible catastrophes we are now so familiar with. Before July and August 1914, European statesmen, especially in central Europe—and there is documentary evidence for this —continually reiterated that peace in Europe was now assured in the long term. The statesmen of central Europe especially used such phrases when speaking to their parties and supporters. I could show you speeches as late as May 1914[30] in which such people said that through the well-ordered diplomatic relations between European countries it was now possible to believe in long-term peace. This was in May 1914! Anyone who saw the real nature of circumstances at the time inevitably spoke differently. Back then, in lectures in Vienna before the war,[31] I expressed thoughts I have often had occasion to utter in recent years: that we are living in something we can only call a cancer of human society, a carcinoma of the social order. This tumour in society erupted and led to the world war.

At the time, because the war had not yet arrived, people naturally thought this idea—that we live in a social tumour or carcinoma—was simply a phrase, a way of speaking. They had no idea as yet that they were perched perilously on a volcano. Nor do they see this now in relation to another potential eruption, truly another such, seething underneath what has long been called the 'social question'. Since people so gladly sleep rather than recognize reality, they fail to see the powers actively at work in this reality, and making it reality.

And that is why it is so difficult to get people today to recognize what is so necessary: to organize society in three distinct spheres if it is to be healthy, to work towards a threefold society. The way of thinking required to recognize this need is different in kind from other ways of thinking. The usual ways of thinking start by trying to work out the best way of ordering society, what ought to be done to achieve this. Please note here the difference between this and the way of thinking that underlies the threefold social organism. The latter does not start by asking what is the best way of organizing society but instead it addresses reality. In other words: how should human beings themselves be freely placed into society and interact with each other to give rise to something healthy? This mode of thinking does not appeal to principles, theories or social dogmas but to the very nature of the human being. It says this: place human beings into the three spheres of society and then these people themselves will dictate how the social order should develop. This is a mode of thinking which appeals to the real nature of humankind rather than to abstract theories or dogmas about how society should be.

If a person lived alone from the beginning, he could never develop the capacity for speech. Human speech can only arise in social community. And someone who lives alone cannot develop any form of social thinking either, no social sense or instinct. Social interactions between people can only develop in the right kind of communal existence. But a great deal now counteracts this socialization in our time. The materialism which has developed in the last few centuries has alienated people from true reality. Human beings have been sundered from it and have grown inwardly lonely. Most lonely of all are those who have become detached from life, torn from its living context, and are now related only to the arid machine, the factory on the one hand, and on the other to soulless capitalism. A wasteland now exists in human souls. Yet from this inner wasteland there struggles free something that can emerge from each individual person: inward thoughts and ideas, inner visions of the supersensible world, visions that also explain outer sensory nature to us. And our loneliness, when we are thrown back entirely on ourselves, is actually the best inner state to recognize our individual relationships with the world of nature and spirit, as opposed to the social thinking that should develop. Only by pondering this will we be able to judge the important historical moment we now find ourselves in. In the course of world evolution human beings had to become lonely enough to seek the life of the spirit in the loneliness of their souls. The loneliest of all have been the great thinkers living in seemingly very abstract heights but who, in their abstractions, were seeking the path to the supersensible world.

Yet we must of course not only seek the path to the supersensible world and to the natural world but also, in our thinking, to the life of society. Since social interaction cannot be developed in loneliness, however, but only in real experience of others, the lonely individual of modern times was not well fitted to develop social thinking. In seeking only to express his inner life, the individual developed anti-social rather than social thinking. We are living, you see, in the most contradictory conditions. Humankind's recent inclinations and longings are an expression of spiritual powers founded on loneliness, but these are powers which the influx of ahrimanic materialism has directed on false paths.

We can fully appreciate the weight and dimensions of this if we ask people what they mean by Bolshevism, which is something that often greatly alarms them. Well, they will reply by speaking of Lenin[32] and Trotsky.[33] In fact there is another figure I could name, who does not belong to our immediate present, and this is none other than the German philosopher Johann Gottlieb Fichte.[34] No doubt you will have heard a thing or two about the ideal, spiritual mode of thinking of Fichte; but it is unlikely that you will have thought of how he expresses himself in human terms even though you may know of the views he recorded in his *The Closed Commercial State*, available for a few pence in the Reclam edition. If you read there how Fichte conceives human assets and commodities, and how he thinks these should be assigned or distributed in the social order, then compare what he says with what Trotsky or Lenin write, you will discover a curious agreement in their views. Then you may well start to see that more is needed than mere outward comparisons and judgements, and you may ask what this is due to. If you study this more closely and try to discover the underlying truth, enquiring into the spiritual orientation found today amongst the most radical figures and theorists, into what, say, unfolds in the soul of Trotsky or Lenin and their particular way of thinking, the forms of their thought, and asking where these could possibly originate, you will discover this: such thinkers are conceivable on the one hand in a different social order, and on the other in this current social order of ours which has developed in the light or rather the darkness of centuries of materialism. Imagine that Lenin and Trotsky emerged in a different social order. What might they have become, do you think, by developing their mental, spiritual powers in a quite different way in different circumstances? They would have become profound mystics! What lives in such souls could for instance become the profoundest mysticism in a religious context and atmosphere, but in the atmosphere of modern materialism it becomes what it has.

If you read Johann Gottlieb Fichte's *The Closed Commercial State*, you find there the social ideal of someone who truly sought to pursue the loftiest paths of knowledge, developing a form of thinking that always inclined towards the supersensible world. He sought to elaborate a social ideal, and this did indeed draw on the purity of the human heart. And yet what fits us to attain the highest ideals of knowledge upon inward paths renders us unfit for developing a social way of thinking if applied to the life of society. In a spiritual nature such as Fichte developed, a person can only pursue his solitary path. Social thinking must be developed in human community; and the thinker's primary task there is to indicate what shape the social organism might take so that people can work together in the right way, embedding social outlooks in society itself. This is why I do not try to tell you, or anyone today, how private ownership of the means of production should be regulated, say, or the common ownership of the means of production. Instead I say this: try to ensure that the social organism is divided into its three spheres, and then whatever is effected or initiated by the flow of capital will be administered from the cultural, spiritual sphere, while all legal parameters will be determined by the political state. Then there will be a proper con-fluence between the life of the legislative state, the cultural, spiritual sphere, and economic life. And then, increasingly, a true social sense will develop which, starting from certain legal concepts, will conduct into the spiritual, cultural organism all we earn that is excess to our own requirements. This will return to the spiritual or cultural organism.

Today such a facility exists only in the sphere of cultural property rights, where no one remarks upon it. One cannot retain cultural property for one's descendants for more than a limited period before it becomes common property—usually 30 years. But this can be a model for giving back to the social organism what has been achieved through individual human capacities, as well as what is subsumed in the capitalist order. The only question then is what sphere this should return to. It should return to the sphere that can properly administer individual spiritual human powers in the right way, or in fact any individual powers and capacities: the spiritual, cultural sphere. People will do this when they stand within the social organism in the right way, and in turn this depends on this way of thinking.

One cannot make any absolute stipulations about these things. But in our time people have become accustomed to viewing everything from a materialistic perspective and therefore they fail to see anything in the right light any more. I have often spoken of how labour has become a commodity in modern times. Ordinary employment contracts do not help here, for they assume labour to be a commodity, and are concluded in relation to work that the worker is obliged to accomplish for the employer. Healthy conditions can only arise if the contract does not govern work at all but if labour is determined as a legal relationship in the rights sphere, that of the political state. The contract is then concluded in relation to distribution of the product created between the person who does the physical work and the one who does the mental or spiritual work. Thus the contract can only govern goods produced and not the relationship between the labourer and the employer. This alone will put things on a sound basis.

But people ask this: what causes the harm in society attaching to capitalism? They reply that this is due to capitalism's economic structures. But in fact this economic order cannot cause harm as such. The harm comes firstly from the fact that there is no real labour law to safeguard work in an appropriate way, and secondly because we do not notice we are living a lie in so far as the worker is denied his full share. But what is this based on? Not on the economic order but on the fact that the social order itself means that the individual capacities of the employer or entrepreneur are not properly shared with the worker. Goods and commodities must be shared since they are produced cooperatively by both the spiritual/mental and physical worker. But what does it mean if, through our individual capacities, we deny or withdraw something from someone which we ought not to? It means that we deceive him, that we exploit him! We have to look at these things squarely and openly. And then we discover that capitalism itself is not at fault but the misuse of spiritual or mental capacities. This relates to our connection with the world of spirit. If you first render the spiritual sphere healthy so that spiritual/mental capacities no longer take undue advantage of those who perform the work, then you make the whole social organism healthy. We have to be able to discern things properly.

But to do so we need some orientation. Today we live in a time when the right orientation can only come from the life of spirit, and therefore our openness to this life of spirit must be a serious practice. Here, repeatedly, we must point out that it is not enough to keep telling people to believe in the spirit. Many 'prophets' are starting to speak of the need for faith in the spirit! Yet it simply is not enough to tell people today, in our current unhealthy conditions, that turning from materialism to the spirit will bring healing. No, mere faith in the spirit will not heal us. Celebrated prophets can trumpet this as much as they like—that modern life has made people superficial and they must now become more inward. These prophets can proclaim that hitherto Christ was only there in people's private lives but now he should enter the life of the state. This achieves absolutely nothing. Today it is not a matter of just believing in the spirit but of filling oneself with spirit to such a degree that we lead this spirit right into outward material reality. Rather than just preaching faith in the spirit, we must speak of a spirit that really masters material reality, that really tells us how to structure the social organism. Today's unspirituality is not due to people's failure to believe in the spirit but to their inability to connect with it in a way that enables it to get to grips with material reality. Lack of belief in the spirit is not due merely to denying this belief but can also be because people assume matter to be merely that, devoid of spirit. Many people today actually think it very refined of themselves to view outward material life as having no spiritual attributes, as something we should withdraw from and turn instead to a rarefied life of spirit. Here we have material reality on the one hand, economic reality, say, where we take care of our pensions or insurance, and on the other hand we enter our meditation chamber and take flight into the spiritual world. Two quite separate currents of life, very nicely sundered! No, that is not the way to live. Instead the spirit needs to become strong enough in our sensibilities for spirit to be more than a sense of personal grace and redemption and to actually intervene in what we seek to do in outer material reality. We have to introduce the spirit, allow it to flow into this outer material reality. To speak of the spirit as a kind of habit is a very easy thing to do; and in this respect many people can find themselves in a strange inner contradiction. Anzengruber's[35] dramatic figure of someone who denies God but affirms this by saying, 'God knows, I am an atheist,' this self-contradictory human figure, does actually exist today albeit in a less crass form than Anzengruber portrays it. This is by no means rare. People often, as it were, swear by God that they have no belief in God.

All this can stand as an admonishment not to look to a mere faith in the spirit but to try, above all, to find the spirit in a way that enables it to strengthen us so that we can really understand material reality. Then people will cease uttering vacuous words about the spirit. Instead, in the very way they look at the world, they will show that they have spiritual insight. That is what we need today: to look at things with spiritual insight rather than just speaking of the spirit. This is important, also to avoid people confusing anthroposophic spiritual science with all the chatter about spirit of which so many are enamoured today. I keep hearing it said of certain worldly preachers of a better kind that their words are 'fully in accord with anthroposophy'. Actually, they are usually saying the opposite! We have to sharpen our vision here, gain clearer insights.

In acknowledging this we will come close to the insight expressed in a sentence by Kurt Eisner, which seems to contain a prescience of his tragic death. This sentence, which I read to you, is especially valuable because it seems to avow that while the person who spoke it does not seriously believe in supersensible reality, or at least will have no recourse to it in his lifetime, there is something worthwhile in the view of those who subscribe to supersensible reality: that sensory existence is a kind of dream, is only half of reality. Eisner seems to say that if we examine the shape this sensory reality has assumed in modern society, it does indeed appear very like a dream and, indeed, like the invention of some evil spirit.

A remarkable avowal. But might we not see things differently? Might it not be true to say that our current tragic, terrible reality originates in the educational intent of a good spirit who prompts us to awaken from an apparent nightmare and seek the full scope of reality, which consists of both sensory and supersensible existence together? We do not have to see our present in nothing but pessi-mistic terms; we can also draw strength from it to affirm this reality. But it will never be enough to see sensory reality as the whole pic-ture. Instead we must find our way from the sensory into the supersensible. Those who do not wish to seek this path would be very short-sighted if they refuse to consider this reality as the invention of an evil spirit. If we develop the will to raise ourselves from this mundane reality into a spiritual reality, however, we will also be able to see that a good spirit is at work. And despite everything that meets our gaze today, we can be sure that human beings will find a way through the tragic destiny of the present. But of course this must include hearkening to the clear need to heal society.

This is what I wished to add today to what I said previously.

LECTURE 5

WE live in a time in which people might recognize, if they wished, what anthroposophic spiritual science has been seeking to achieve for many years. It would actually be the very finest fruit of anthroposophic endeavour if, in the hearts and souls of those involved in this movement, a conviction could arise that the fiery signs of our time offer proof of the need for these long-term endeavours. Whatever turbulent outward events occur in the world, whatever form is taken by things seeking to work their way out of the underdepths of human evolution, we only really hearken to the true, underlying nature of these events—which escapes the notice of ordinary human perception—if we observe the world from a spiritual perspective.

I would like to start today with one such phenomenon, which is scarcely noticed under the tumult of events. It is regarded as something unimportant and of little concern, yet those who have drawn on spiritual foundations to acquire an ability to see life's reality will accord it all due weight.

For the past seven or eight years—this may sound paradoxical but it is true—children have been born with a quite different countenance from before. People fail to notice it, giving little heed to such things—giving little heed, in fact, to all the most important things in life. But if you have acquired the ability to observe such things, you will know that the faces of children born during the past seven, eight or even ten years betray something lacklustre, like a wariness towards the world. We can discern this in the physiognomy of newborn children from the very first days after birth, and this is different from before. If we study this curious phenomenon, which may sound very paradoxical to people today, we find that the souls of children who have entered the world at birth, who pass through conception and birth, already bear with them something that gives their countenance a melancholic stamp, however much they smile. The faces of newborn infants used not to bear this quality. And in their souls, quite unconsciously of course, lives a mood of reluctance to enter life. The souls being born today—as I said, this has been true for around ten years now—feel something like a hindrance and constraint in entering this physical world.

Before we enter the physical world, passing through conception and birth, we experience an important occurrence in the world of spirit which then shines its light ahead of it and has effects in the forthcoming life. Here on earth people die, pass through the portal of death, lay aside their physical body and bring their souls into the world of spirit. The soul still bears within it the effects of all it experienced here in the physical world. In passing through the gate of death, basically the soul looks like these effects themselves, like the experiences it underwent in earthly life. Having crossed the threshold of death, these souls encounter the souls who are preparing to descend into a physical body. This occurrence is a reality that I can only describe to you because it is available to the seer's experience and perception. It is an important thing, this encounter between the souls of those who have just died and those who will soon enter the physical world through the portal of birth: it sets a tone. In a sense it infuses descending souls with an idea of what they might meet here. This encounter gives rise to the impulse that impresses an odd melancholy on the faces of infants from birth. They do not really wish to enter the world they have learned of through this encounter, for they are aware that their 'spiritual plumage' will be badly ruffled by experiences of a humanity plunged in a materialistic view of the world, and immersed also in materialistic actions. This encounter, which of course we can only ascertain spiritually, also sheds a strong light on our whole modern era, which we can only properly understand by acknowledging such hidden phenomena. Yet this is something we must try to understand.

This is something, to start with, that can of course only be perceived through spiritual vision. But other phenomena today speak loud and clear to us, and could be discernible without spiritual vision for anyone who does not sleepwalk through life. The global catastrophe of the past four or five years has had its dire impact on the world; and we keep looking back—as I think every wakeful soul must do today—to the palpable, perceptible origins of this terrible human catastrophe. We study the course it has taken and, finally, can examine what has emerged from it now on a worldwide scale. Here one thing ought to be apparent for anyone who is awake. Take the curious fact that this world war broke over central Europe and yet—and this is true—no one wishes to know what really gave rise to it. People wonder what its origins were, blame this party or that, but ultimately, whatever blame they assign, come to the conclusion that this was not the whole cause, that other factors must have been at work too.

People say that a great social movement emerged from this catastrophic world war. Whether partisan or not, they try to understand what should now be done in these great social upheavals. And yet their thoughts relate to reality as an embalmed body does to life. Their mummified thoughts are not adequate to grapple with the turbulence of events, with its real nature. If we study these things more closely, now that a series of memoirs have been published by figures directly involved in the origins of the world war, we have to ask whether these people really took part in the events of four or five years ago that they describe. Did they really know what they were doing? Did they have any inkling of the scope of what their rational minds concocted? Increasingly it must become apparent that they did not, as we see from the confession of Russian minister Sukhomlinov.[36] In his court testimony, in relation to the three or four hours during which he had to make his most vital decisions, he said that he must have lost his mind, that he must have been mad!

Such phenomena tell us a great deal. They indicate that mental confusion reigned in the minds of many of those involved. Anyone equipped to see into the terrible nature of current world events will see—and increasingly people *will* see this—that the events originated less in moral failure than in an intellectual inability to understand world events. Things are still the same today. The majority of people are, basically, helpless in the face of these world events, and we have to ask, very seriously indeed, what this is due to. There is an underlying factor here that is extraordinarily difficult for our time to grasp, pervaded as it is by a materialistic outlook. Since the turning point in world history when the materialistic world-view reached its highest tide, the strongest spiritual power that has ever sought to enter human life from the world of spirit is seeking entry. This is the characteristic nature of our time. Since the beginning of the last third of the nineteenth century, the spirit, the world of spirit, is seeking to reveal itself to humankind in the strongest possible way. Yet human beings have gradually reached a point in their evolution where they wish only to use the tool of their physical body to grasp anything. In their materialistic outlook they have become accustomed to asserting the theory that the physical brain is the tool for thinking, and even for feeling and will. They have persuaded themselves that the physical body is the tool for all spiritual and mental activity. It is not without reason that they have done so, for as human evolution progressed people indeed gradually reached a state where they can only use the physical body as a tool for mental activity. Today therefore we find ourselves in the midst of a vitally important knot in human evolution, where the world of spirit seeks to reveal itself as if in tempest and turbulence, and on the other hand people must find the strength to free themselves from the warp of materialism and work their way through to new receptivity to spiritual revelations.

Today humanity faces the greatest test of its powers, that of working its way freely and independently towards the spirit, which will itself approach us if we do not close ourselves off from it. But the time is now past when the spirit could reveal itself to us in all kinds of subconscious and unconscious processes. The time has come when we must receive the light of spirit in our own free, inward deed. And all the confusion and unclarity which people live in today is due to the fact they now need to receive something which they do not yet wish to receive: an entirely new understanding of things.

Old forms of thinking, the old way of surveying world events, came to expression in this dire, terrible world war. This catastrophe, with its hugely significant symptoms of coming disaster, is urging us to think differently, to seek new ways of seeing the world, since the old ways will end only in chaos and confusion. We must, finally, come to see that the leading figures in 1914 had arrived at a point where nothing more could be achieved through old kinds of comprehension, and that this is why they led humanity into misfortune. Today people must inscribe this knowledge deep in their hearts, for otherwise they will not take the strong resolve to approach the living spirit out of their own free, inner powers. In our immediate present, most worryingly, things are coming to expression that cannot be understood by means of the old world-views and outlooks on life. And yet people still cling to them and refuse to entertain quite new ways of perceiving and thinking. The anthroposophic world-view has sought to prepare humanity to develop these new forms of seeing the world. The opposition to it has really been nothing other than people's inner sluggishness and laziness, the inability to collect the inmost powers of their soul and bring these towards the wave of spirit breaking upon us now so mightily.

I said earlier that people accustomed themselves to using only their physical body in thinking, and this eventually led to the materialistic world-view. Now there is something that it is essential to understand in our time. Nature can be understood by the methods which science is so triumphant about, by using the instrument of the physical brain, the physical body altogether. But this instrument is not adequate for understanding human life. We can only comprehend it if we can raise ourselves to a form of thinking not drawn entirely from the physical body alone—and this can be cultivated through the anthroposophic world-view. Of course people say they don't understand anthroposophic books and lectures, the world-view enshrined there. I can well believe it. But what does this failure to understand mean? It means simply that I wish only to use my physical brain to understand the world, that I do not wish to learn to think in any other way than by lazily settling back in the comfortable armchair of the physical brain. It is absolutely true that the anthroposophic world-view cannot be understood by those means. It is not that one has to be clairvoyant to understand it, but one does have to practise a form of thinking not bound to the physical brain. The content of anthroposophic literature, which can be comprehended with healthy common sense, gradually schools a kind of thinking, feeling and will that is equal to today's tumultuous events. You can take this as you like, but it is true: the present day asks us no longer to grasp the world through the instrument of the physical body but through the instrument of the etheric body—the level of our being which, as a body of formative forces, underlies and sustains the physical body.

The great influx of spirit seeking to reveal itself to humanity comes to expression really only in very unconscious feelings in people, and they have an awful fear of it. Actually, when people say they don't understand spiritual science, this is only an excuse. The truth is they are afraid of the revelations of the world of spirit, and it is only because they do not wish to acknowledge this fear that they say spiritual science is incomprehensible to them, or else that it is illogical or some other evasion. In truth they are afraid of it and therefore resort to anything that enables them not to face the great and pressing problems of our time. How happy they are when they can evade the great tasks and riddles of modern life! They find it uncomfortable to hear about various urgent problems in the world today, although they quite happily attend plays by Ibsen where some of these problems come to light.[37] But since this is just 'art' they do not feel prompted to further concern. People find it uncomfortable to hear directly of the influx of the world of spirit into mundane reality.

Bjørnson[38] too included such themes in his plays, and these could likewise be dismissed as merely aesthetic matters. People had an awful fear of addressing these things seriously, but all the while class conflicts were increasing, a gulf opening between the ruling classes and the proletariat. The social question presented riddles, and this was regarded as an uncomfortable subject for discussion. Yet people went to the theatre and watched Hauptmann's *The Weavers*,[39] got a little inwardly exercised about the depths of human depravity portrayed there but not seriously enough to take a stance on such matters: it was, after all, 'just art'. They escaped into something they did not need to take seriously, a characteristic trait in the contemporary psyche. And what underlies this characteristic phenomenon? That, given the revelations of the world of spirit, they needed to try to take certain things seriously which cannot be comprehended by means of the instrument of the physical body alone, which can only be understood through imaginative powers in the same way that art itself can only be understood in this way. The human physical body is a product of nature while the human etheric body is like a work of art in form and pattern, really like a sculpture, except that it is in continual movement. What people otherwise accept in their enjoyment of art has to consolidate, grow brighter and become serious vision: Imagination, Inspiration, Intuition. And then people will understand what is trying to reveal itself to them today. Behind events, you see, lurks something that can only be spiritually comprehended. We must develop a deep awareness, a real feeling, that what is seeking to enter the contemporary world as spiritual revelation can only be comprehended through spiritual science itself, that is, through thinking, feeling and inner impulses of will that can be schooled through the science of the spirit, and which unfold in the same region of life that artistic endeavour occupies, albeit often as mere reflection without serious content.

A good many years ago, in a particular field, I tried to point to something that is of urgent necessity today. Naturally it was not understood by the banal and philistine monstrosity that is called academia. My *Philosophy of Freedom*, published in 1894, contained a chapter entitled 'Moral Imagination'. In terms of spiritual science we could also say, 'imaginative moral impulses'. I tried to show that the domain which is otherwise only imaginatively comprehended in art must now necessarily be taken up seriously by humanity, since this is the level which people must attain in order to allow supersensible reality to inform them in a way the physical brain cannot grasp. At least in relation to our grasp of morality, in the early 1890s I sought to show that comprehending the supersensible is an important and serious matter. We should have a sense of these things today: of the fact that thoughts, inner soul impulses which came to expression in the catastrophic world war and have continued into this time of social upheavals are of no use any more; that we need new impulses. But if one tries to introduce a new impulse today, this meets with incomprehension, for it is one drawn livingly from the world of spirit as a remedy to heal the disorders of our time. And in response to such a thing, people on both left and right squeak in dismay; from one political extreme to the other they are united in a common chorus that this is not something they can fathom. Of course they can't if they wish to stay with their old, outmoded forms of thinking. This we should do no longer, but instead should reconfigure and reform our inner apprehension entirely. All outward revolutions—however much they accord with the desires of any party or class of society— will lead us up the creek and bring dire misery over humanity if they are not illumined by an inner revolution in the soul, by a will to depart from immersion in a purely materialistic world-view and open ourselves to the spiritual wave seeking to break over humanity as a new revelation. The revolution from matter to spirit is the only wholesome revolution, while all others are like childhood diseases— like scarlet fever, measles—and mere preliminaries to the re-establishment of a new health implicit in the emergence of spirit in modern life.

Today we need a strong inner resolve if we are to be equal to what the times are asking of us. We should give full, serious credence to the reality of a world of spirit that seeks to break through into our own. Powers of spirit truly exist and we should found our decisions, actions and our whole thinking on them. This is what is being asked of us! Much is in flux and change at such times. And here I would like to point to another symptom that will again sound paradoxical but which, perceived inwardly, spiritually, is of the very greatest importance. As you know from your studies of spiritual science, apart from our physical body and our etheric body—which I mentioned just now as an instrument we need to spiritually comprehend what may otherwise remain a mere reflection of reality in art—we also have our soul nature as such. We can call this the astral body or whatever name you like. It is substantially more spiritual than the etheric body and therefore is something from which, during the period of materialistic developments, people were still further removed than from the etheric body. You see, underlying the physical body, the etheric body has a kind of shape and form albeit one in continual motion, while the astral body is intrinsically formless. In speaking of it, we are speaking really only pictorially, in a metaphor, a picture that only represents what we are referring to, since it has no form as such. Over the past three to four hundred years this astral body has changed a great deal in modern humanity. In the past the astral body was still relatively permeated, pervaded, interwoven by all kinds of spiritual forces; and human beings' spiritual feelings and impulses still originated in this spiritual immanence within the astral body. Now, by contrast, human astral bodies have really become empty, since the power of the world of spirit is seeking in a sense to approach from without and reveal itself, and so we must absorb this outer, spiritual world into us. And therefore our astral body has gradually become empty, and must now begin to fill again with the revelations approaching it from without. This has a very specific effect on people. And now I come to the thing which—as I said— will seem very paradoxical, just as much so as the melancholic countenance of children born today. But it is true nevertheless.

The most important occurrence in the origins of the First World War,[40] in so far as this concerns events in Berlin, occurred on 1 August between the afternoon and the evening, roughly between a quarter to four in the afternoon and eleven or twelve at night.

Various people were involved, naturally people belonging to our materialistic era. This time of day is the least favourable for human decisions to be made if they are embedded in a materialistic outlook. You see, we have entered a very, very important stage in human evolution. People today cannot make good decisions if—however strange this seems—they do not wake up with them in the morning. Increasingly humankind will come to recognize the truth of this, dawning on them even through external realities. On awakening, a person may not be aware of such a decision, but in his subconscious he undergoes in the night something he can then experience next morning. People have not yet reached the stage of being able to prefigure things prophetically, though that is not the important thing. But if you harbour a thought at around half-past three in the afternoon, or six in the evening, it may be one you had in the night, that has now reawoken in you. If a thought occurs to you that did not form in the night, and by contrast is drawn from the events of the day, this will not be good or useful nowadays. People today need to draw their most important impulses from the world of spirit, for these cannot be found in the physical world at all. Today we are in a sense obliged to be unreasonable if we do not already bring our decisions and resolves with us, if we do not appeal to this coexistence with the world of spirit. The essential thing occurs at night when our astral body is freed from the physical and etheric body and, outside them, is together with the world of spirit; then, more than was the case with our ancestors, it is prepared for the reason and decisions of the day. This is why the moment of awakening should be sacred to modern people. We should sense that we emerge then from the world of spirit and enter the physical world. And everything good, all that enables me to be a reasonable person, I gain by my interactions with the world of spirit while I am asleep, by my dialogue with the dead whom I knew when they were alive and who have died before me—in brief, through what I experience in communion with those who are no longer in a physical body when I am with them at night in the pure world of spirit. And out of this experience in the spiritual realm I should develop within me an underlying sense of the sacredness of the moment of awakening. Then this underlying feeling will infuse my day with an ability to say, of one event, that a spiritual impulse will help me here, and of another that nothing can help me at present, it must remain unresolved, and I will have to wait for a new day to dawn to resolve it.

This is a way of living with a spiritual orientation, really counting on spiritual factors. In our materialistic age people of course do not count on spiritual factors. Instead they believe themselves to be 'clever'. They believe that they have all they need for this cleverness in the instrument of the physical brain. They do not appeal to what they can acquire in the condition of separation from the physical world, when they are one with the world of spirit in their astral body. The only thing that can give true health back to humanity is the will to lead a spiritual life, to allow spiritual resolves, spiritual impulses to inform what we do in the physical realm.

This is something people ought to give full and thorough consideration to today. You see, the anthroposophic world-view cannot involve just absorbing a sum of abstract concepts as a kind of catechism, an abstract doctrine, and then feeling pleased that our world-view is different from that of others. No. The anthroposophic world-view must change the very nature of our thinking, the hue of our feeling; it must enable that great moment of awakening in spirit to occur and teach us that we must allow the spirit to illumine our life. The misfortune of modern humanity arose because the will's refusal to absorb spiritual content was driven to its furthest extreme. Never before has such an event as this catastrophic world war arisen from such outward factors, such purely material imperatives, and for that very reason it assumed such terrible proportions. Humankind should learn from this that its past thinking, feeling and will has driven it into this catastrophe, and that we will not emerge from it— although it will assume different and diverse forms—until, with a keen power of resolve, we undertake to transform ourselves inwardly, to seek the metamorphosis of our soul.

The realities I have described to you are just that, realities: the melancholic cast in children's faces, the need to use our etheric body to comprehend the world, and the need for our will impulses to appeal, at the moment of awakening, to the glowing embers in us, if you will, of what remains with us from the sleep we have just had. This invitation to the spirit to speak in us will grow ever more vital as humanity evolves. We must grasp the fact that the anthroposophic world-view does not aim to be mere sensation for lazy souls, which is what modern mystics often are, that it is not some kind of icing on the cake of life, an outward, physical delectation, but instead something inwardly bound up with the deepest impulses in culture. Likewise we should recognize that our culture cannot grow healthy if not rendered fruitful by the anthroposophic world-view. This should be inscribed deeply in the souls of those who have become acquainted with this outlook.

Thus I wanted today to characterize one aspect of the decisive moment in world evolution in which humanity currently finds itself. Of course, if one adopts contemporary views, it is easy to judge as idiocy the things it is most necessary to say. People believe they are Christians, and yet they have not begun to understand the saying which tells us that human wisdom is often folly before God,[41] and that all folly, and perhaps stupidity as it appears to human beings, may well be wisdom before God. In the same way people today so easily forget the inward impulses underlying reality and hold fast instead to empty phrases. Today it is thought that a sermon is 'Christian' simply because the word 'Christ' or 'Jesus' figures in it repeatedly, never mind that the actual content of what is said is not Christian at all. By contrast, if you seek to promulgate what Christ lays in our souls today, and in doing so hearken to the Old Testament saying, applicable also to Christianity, that 'Thou shalt not take the name of the Lord in vain', people think what you say cannot be Christian. People reel off the Ten Commandments like parrots, and repeatedly utter the name of their God in vain, yet think the very speaking of this name makes them especially Christian. Similarly we are not thought to be good Germans if we don't keep saying the word 'German'. It is vital today to recognize that the deepest powers of German culture have actually been trodden underfoot in the past

30 years, and can only be resuscitated again through spiritual contemplation, spiritual deepening.

Looking towards the West we find a culture in the process of making itself entirely materialistic, but which nevertheless has a certain inner, instinctive assurance and therefore cannot succumb entirely to materialism. Then we look towards the East and find a culture that abhors everything western, including us, since this eastern culture is still embedded in an older, ancient spirituality, and in a sense is in the process of renewing it. Midway between these two, it is our task to find the right path between western materialism on the one hand and eastern spirituality on the other, since the latter is not appropriate for us. Here, at the centre of Europe, we should become aware of our great responsibility, at the same time acknowledging that we have, to a very great degree, lost sight of this sense of responsibility in recent decades. What has the life of spirit, cultural life, become? A mere appendage to the state, an appendage to economic life. When the state administers cultural life, especially education, this spells its ruination. We need a free spiritual and cultural life, for what the world of spirit seeks to reveal to humanity can only flow through the veins of a free cultural life. This wave, this surge of spiritual life has to descend amongst us! It will never, ever reveal itself to those who are hamstrung as servants of the state, state officials, or who, even in cultural life, are beholden to economic life. It will reveal itself only to those who are immersed in the free life of spirit and culture, those who daily wrestle with the life of spirit. The times themselves are asking for spiritual, cultural life to be freed from its bondage to state and economy.

These things which, in another form, are propounded today as the 'threefolding of the social organism'[42] are in fact Christianity: spiritual revelations clothed in outward forms. They are what humanity needs, what alone can offer a sound foundation and the real possibility to change our thinking, to relearn what humanity so urgently needs. We have been compelled to wage war with a country that possesses a very highly developed instinctive political life, with many established colonies, along with colony-related industrialization. We waged war as a country whose industrialism is still emergent, that was still seeking to acquire colonies. Instead we should have invoked spirit in these endeavours. What has occurred in Germany in the economic life of the past 30 years has been the very greatest disservice to the spirit: a programme that rejected spiritual, cultural life, that entrusted itself to random chance, random unspiritual accident. It is as if the spirit of the cosmos, by laying the greatest trial on the German people, wished to teach it something vital: that nothing can work without the spirit, and that this nation must realize this. Yet it seems the Germans are very reluctant to embrace this insight since they still appear willing to condemn anything and everything other than their lack of sense of responsibility towards the spirit. Today we are witnessing this complete failure of awareness or self-reflection amongst people, very unqualified for this, to whom the West has entrusted governance of the destiny of the German people. The whole undertaking of those involved in this is nonsensical; there is no will to examine things properly, to look at what is really happening, and this testifies still to sleepwalking souls. They should long since have said that what happened at Versailles, what they agreed to there, is completely unfit and inadequate to meet the current world-historical situation. But these things can only properly be judged when one develops awareness of responsibility towards the spirit, acknowledging that this is indeed a vital moment in world history, and that one has a responsibility therefore not to regard things superficially as usual, but to accord them their full importance. In certain fields today you can talk until the cows come home but it will do no good, and so people find it easier to shrug their shoulders and leave it to those in charge—whether the old aristocrats, decadent aristocrats, or Marxists. The latter know least of all what is needed, may at the most have read a little of Marx's *Das Kapital*,[43] but if they do not find the will to accomplish the great transformation of soul which could enable them to think in new ways, nothing good will come of it. The revolution of 9 November 1918[44] was not one, for what changed then was only skin-deep. All that changed, really, was that those who bore office were replaced by others who now bear office instead. We have to look deeper, but to do so we need to think, and to think we need good will—which arises only if we school it through preoccupation with the world of spirit. It is this preoccupation with the spiritual world which is the real balm needed to heal humanity today, the only effective one.

Given this opportunity to speak together again today, this is what I wished to present to you in relation to contemporary events, as these inevitably appear to me. I offered these thoughts in the hope that increasingly in our anthroposophic movement, and in ever wider and wider circles, people will endeavour not only to secure inner comfort and peace of mind but also develop something that can bear fruit for the whole cultural life of humanity.

I am very pleased indeed to see how many more friends, members of our anthroposophic movement, are sitting here now than were here a year ago. May the spirit so resonant in the modern world and in humanity's evolution help increase the number of our friends to the same or to an even greater extent every year. The more human souls upon whom this spirit impresses a conviction of the need for new thinking, feeling and will, and for a new sense of responsibility, the better it will be for the world.

LECTURE 6

BERLIN, 12 SEPTEMBER 1919

TODAY, the first time I have spoken to you about anthroposophic matters here in this space,[45] I wish first of all to express my gratitude to the friends who, while I was away from Berlin, put such devoted effort into preparing these premises to serve our anthroposophic reflections and work. We live in a time when the human soul must engage with great, encompassing events in the cosmos and in human evolution. If we seek to fully understand our place as human beings in the world, these great, far-reaching events require our keen will to such an extent that we cannot so easily attend to outer beauty, such as the furnishing of these rooms, as perhaps we did in former, calmer, or at least seemingly calmer times. These rooms are to be dedicated to ideal goals, spiritual goals, and here people can work together socially and communally. But if we reflect a little we can see that there is a certain connection between the great events pulsing through the world today and premises such as these. The significant demands which human history and evolution now make upon us will, after all, increasingly tend towards the transformation of a past aesthetic—in which human beings sought beauty in and for their own private and egoistic enjoyment—towards spaces and dimensions in which they collaborate socially. We do not properly judge the future aims seeking to unfold in human evolution if we see them in terms of the cultural phenomena sometimes apparently surfacing today. The social movement of today bears, apparently, a 'more democratic' character, though we need only grasp its transient nature to discern what is inherent in this movement, and recognize its true characteristics. At the same time, this movement also bears in it something that could strike alarm into us: it seems that the aesthetic beauty, the art which is such a part of our earthly culture, will not meet in future with the same understanding as in the past when materially prosperous circles had the luxury of devoting themselves to the pursuit of beauty.

A time of transition may lead to aesthetic sensitivity receding somewhat. But precisely when our life assumes more social forms and dimensions, it will be indispensible that outward spatial forms are aesthetically informed by the character and needs of the times, for otherwise humanity would succumb to philistine banality. Thus the simple beauty in which our friends sought to express the serious tenor of matters to be aired here in future is something we can see as symbolic of the great events that pulse through our times. And I believe I speak for all of you when, with such feelings, I offer my warmest thanks at this grave time for the work our friends have accomplished here. It would also be wrong to believe that developments in preparation today are such that 'objective events' in the world might lead to a diminution of the value of individual, personal attributes and all that originates in them. This is not so. It is only during the centuries up to the end of the nineteenth, the last three to four centuries, that it has appeared justified in terms of overall human evolution to see the human being as a cog in the universal mechanism. In the near future it will be a human task to work our way out of this universal mechanism again. And therefore we can certainly say that the great movement of the present day has a mostly egoistic character, is thoroughly egoistic. Yes, people strive for socialism, but they do so out of entirely anti-social drives and instincts. We should not overlook this—that today we strive for socialism, basically, because people have grown so inwardly anti-social. If the social instinct were more self-evident we would not need so many social programmes, which have arisen only as a reaction to our anti-social feelings.

But precisely in such an era when things remain so muddled and unclear, when a social element is seeking to be born out of egoism and anti-social instincts, a very particular effect emanates from what has been accomplished through noble, selfless dedication to an ideal, sustained by authentic, true, unegoistic human feelings. And it will be good if we celebrate this in a sense, though not in an external way, by turning our thoughts in these grave times to an appreciation of what I have just expressed: to the great value of finding, alongside the rampant egoism of our time, a means to create what has been created here, albeit in very limited scope, in the form of ideal, spiritual work. Today it seems to me that the most festive means of celebrating this is to engage in reflections which address the seriousness of the times, on the one hand, so that this sense of seriousness can invoke feelings in our soul that accompany us in the work to be undertaken here in these rooms, for as long as these times continue to allow this work here; and on the other, to keep allowing thoughts to work upon us which, because so intimately connected with humanity's evolution, can be worthy of our inner contemplation whenever we enter these premises to fulfil the tasks that they aim to serve.

If we give critical attention to our time—but not critical in a disparaging sense—we cannot help but see, if we are honest, the numerous signs and currents of decline apparent in every sphere of life. If we are not to lose our sense of seriousness we must not forget what a gulf commonly exists between the usual content of people's awareness, to which they give verbal expression, and all that is inwardly true and real. Broad swathes of the population today have lost any sense or feeling that the words we speak are so often far removed from the truth. An elemental outflow of truth from the human soul has, one can say, been replaced by generalized phrases. Empty phrases are best characterized as speech not inwardly con-nected with the source of truth—and the connection can after all only be an inward one. We need only consider the manifestations of general untruth that have surfaced in the world over the past four or five years and we will see beyond doubt that in departing so generally

from authentic reality people have instead come to express themselves in empty phrases, in formulaic utterances. If nothing were to
counteract this, the trend would keep increasing. In modern times,
along with such phrase-mongering, great indulgence has developed
towards this untruthfulness, a kind of easy tolerance of it and
inclination for it. Wherever people speak empty phrases you find also
a great tolerance of it and of the untruth it embodies. Those who
tolerate it so easily ascribe the best intentions to those who speak it;
and there is very little conscientious sense of truth which would
require someone who opens his mouth to examine the basis of what
he says and to refrain from speaking until he has done so. The time
must come when it is no longer sufficient to say that someone who
says something untrue is well-meaning. We must instead develop a
very sharp sense of responsibility towards the truth, towards testing
and verifying it, realizing that we should not merely be lenient with
ourselves when we discover that something we said in good faith does
not correspond to reality. We need to realize that as far as objective
knowledge of the world is concerned our subjective belief that we
have spoken the truth is not what counts, and that for this objective
world knowledge it does indeed matter whether we say something
objectively true, that corresponds to reality, or something that is not
and does not. Specifically because of these grave times we will have to
learn the difference between true utterance and empty phrase.

Nowadays, though they are not fully conscious of this, people have
a feeling that they can say whatever they feel like. You can see this,
and I have studied it, in the stance people take towards contemporary events. We have overlooked things of great seriousness,
which people judge only as they are inclined to rather than according
to the real significance of these events for humanity's whole evolution. In our midst have been figures directly involved in and
responsible for what has happened over the past four to five years—
people whom circumstances have placed in prime positions in
relation to global events. The destiny of these people has now
overtaken them! But very few are willing to seek an objective
judgement of what has actually happened, to ask by what means, by

what kinds of choice and selection, these leading figures secured their leading positions and wrought the disaster that they did. Nothing is more important today than to wrestle our way through all subjective opinions to find a certain objectivity in respect of these things. Many people think it is an easy matter today to speak the truth. It is not easy, since truth has so many enemies and because those who do speak it are quickly marginalized. You will often court disfavour if you speak the truth today.

In recent months, when it was so often said to me that the ideas I expressed about society were so hard to comprehend, that people could not grasp what I meant, I repeatedly countered this by saying that comprehension of this social impulse required a different mood of soul than that prevailing in central Europe over the past four or five years, or culminating then and in fact already present long before. Over these four to five years people have understood a great deal—have understood things that I, certainly, did not understand. Many figures have made all sorts of statements and declamations, beautifully couched and framed, but an honest sense of truth could make nothing of them, though people seemed to comprehend them. They did so because they were ordered to. When orders came from the HQ of war operations they understood them. But now we need to understand things that we are not commanded to, that we grasp by our own free, inner capacities. Perhaps people have now lost the habit of this and will have to reacquire it. The past four or five years have truly shown that these capacities are lacking and must be regained. Habits that have developed in recent years oblige us to counter them with the truth, and this is no pleasant duty firstly because the truth is a serious matter and secondly because you are often much frowned on for speaking it.

There will come a time when people look back on these times of ours in a very particular way. Our obligations have altered from what they were only quite recently, and therefore one now has to give people an idea of how future times will judge what is occurring now.

They will have to learn to turn their gaze, their spiritual gaze, once more to the great shifts occurring, to the great developmental impulses now affecting humanity on the earth. One such transformative impulse began in the mid-fifteenth century, and we refer to this in our anthroposophic spiritual science as the beginning of the fifth post-Atlantean epoch. We know that this is quite different in character from the former Graeco-Roman epoch, which began in the eighth century BC and ended in the fifteenth century AD. Immersed in the *fable convenue* that people call history, they do not discern the huge difference in the mood of the human soul between, say, the tenth century and the centuries that began around the middle of the fifteenth. New outlooks, a new atmosphere of soul came upon humanity then, and we can only really understand these developments and transformations if we turn our inner gaze upwards to the powers that hold sway in humanity, which for instance played into these upheavals and new impulses in the middle of the fifteenth century. In our own time, now that several centuries have passed since the mid-fifteenth century, what broke over human civilization back then has in a sense culminated in a crisis. It slowly developed until our own time, reaching a decisive point today, a key moment that human consciousness must grasp.

We have reached a point when human beings must become aware—how they will do this is something we will speak further of—that they stand here within earthly occurrences, and besides them there are three realms of nature: the animal, plant and mineral kingdoms. But in acknowledging this from the perspective of modern consciousness of the fifth post-Atlantean epoch we state only half the truth. People living before this epoch spoke the whole truth when they said this since they understood things differently. They saw spirit at work in these animal, plant and mineral kingdoms, whereas people today have lost this awareness; they must regain it by developing the insight that just as they are connected with the three kingdoms below them, so also they are connected above them with the three realms of the Angeloi, Archangeloi and Archai. Just as our physical body has a certain relationship with the animal, plant and mineral kingdoms, so our soul and spirit are related to the nature of these three heavenly hierarchies. A time has arrived when, just as our relationship with the three natural kingdoms has undergone great changes, so we are likewise changing our relationship with the three realms of the hierarchies above us. Today I want to speak to you about this serious aspect of humanity's evolution, acknowledgement of which is the most fitting and festive way to celebrate the inauguration of these new premises.

If we look back to what happened in human evolution in previous epochs ending around the middle of the fifteenth century—and for now leaving higher hierarchies to one side—we have to say that the beings of the Angeloi, Archangeloi and the Archai have always been preoccupied with the human being in so far as he passes through an existence between death and a new birth, and also an existence between birth and death here on the earthly plane. But in our era, this preoccupation of the beings of these three hierarchies with the human being in a sense came to a conclusion. The manifold activities which the beings of these three hierarchies were obliged to undertake included this: to collaborate on the image underlying the physical human being on earth, his physical organization. At birth we enter upon physical existence and grow within earthly conditions, a process during which the image of humanity, of humankind, comes to expression in us. In ancient times this human image was very different, and has undergone much change. You need only remember what emerges when we look back to ancient Atlantean times, or even just back to Egyptian culture; people were different in their outward form and structure. The image of the human being has changed, and the task of the beings of these three higher hierarchies was to work upon it. Their tasks included elaborating this image, developing it from what it was in ancient Lemuria, then Atlantis, through to what it became in the various post-Atlantean epochs. Thus the beings of these three higher hierarchies gradually created the image that now underlies the earthly human being through transformation from more ancient images.

But here we come to the remarkable thing, revealed to a truly spiritual observation of human evolution. In our age, these three hierarchies have now largely concluded the fundamental development of this human image. In so far as it underlies the human physical organism, this image of humankind is finished and complete. Try to gain a feeling for this significant fact: the beings of the hierarchies, the Angeloi, Archangeloi and Archai, have worked upon the human image through many, many millennia, and this image is the foundation and pattern, if you like, of our human physical organization. And now we live in an age when these beings of the three higher hierarchies say to themselves, 'We have worked upon the image of humankind but now this work is done. We have placed the human being into this earthly world as physical entity, and this work is now finished.'

In studying this fact through spiritual vision we can be struck and shaken to discover that the interest of the beings of these three higher hierarchies in creating this physical image has not only lessened in our age but disappeared entirely. If we look back to the Graeco-Roman period, these beings of the higher hierarchies still had a lively interest in creating this image of the physical human being on earth, whereas now their interest is gone. Their feeling is that they have done their part on behalf of the physical human being on earth, and from this perspective their interest has faded altogether. We human beings can regard this as an especially significant fact with decisive effects on human nature. To realize its scope people need only take the time and leisure to observe the outward characteristics of humankind's evolution. If we look back to former times we can tell from much that has occurred and has been passed down to us that certain thoughts surfaced instinctively in people of earlier times. Those in whom certain thoughts surface instinctively in this way are regarded as geniuses. Or at least it is believed that this happens still today, but there is little of genius left in human beings on earth. You see, the forces of genius no longer surface from the body's organism since the beings of the three higher hierarchies no longer work upon this organism. They have lost interest in the corporeal form of the human being.

In certain respects the fact that the form of the human body is now finished renders modern human beings arrogant. Throughout the rest of earthly evolution we will no longer perfect our physical earthly form. No further perfecting of our organism will occur in corporeal terms. What once surfaced instinctively as the traits of genius in the human soul arose from the body and at the same time, because it was the work of gods, exerted an organizing effect on the body. When Homer created his epics, for instance, his poetry drew on a power which in the ancient Greeks was at the same time an organizing power that shaped and configured the Greek body. Emerging with tangible force and momentum, this simultaneously had body-forming powers. By contrast, the laws of nature we deduce today, of which we are so proud, are largely abstractions and have no power to shape and configure the body. We therefore form abstract thoughts that are unable to exert a mastering influence on society, and abstract laws of nature. And this is because the beings of the three higher hierarchies no longer work upon us, and therefore thoughts with organizing power no longer surface within us. Our being of soul has grown abstract. The soul within our body has been forsaken by the activity, the work, of the beings of the three higher hierarchies.

And here we come to the important thing: that we must now seek through our own resources to connect again with the work of the beings of the three higher hierarchies. Hitherto, these beings came towards us, worked upon us. Now we ourselves must work upon our own soul and spirit. And the soul-spiritual work we accomplish, what we reveal of the world of spirit through spiritual-scientific research, will become in our human soul something that rekindles the interest of these hierarchical beings. They will be in the thoughts and feelings we draw from the world of spirit, and by this means we will again forge a connection with the beings of the hierarchies. That is the degree of significance of what is happening today: we must see it as a change in the relationship between the world of gods and human-kind. Until our own times, gods worked to perfect the physical human image; and now human beings must start to work upon the content of their soul so that they find the way back to the three higher hierarchies. One of the great difficulties of our age is that people are so proud of their now perfected external, corporeal image,

and develop abstract thoughts independently of it, that is, independently of any higher world; these thoughts have no connection
with the world of spirit. And yet our proper task now is really to seek
this connection by our own resources, through dedication to spiritual
knowledge, through feelings about spiritual knowledge, and by
drawing our impulses of will from spiritual knowledge. Only
through a full, feeling awareness of this great change in evolution—
though it takes place over centuries—can one find the right outlook
in our era. We cannot find our place in this era through merely
external reflections, but must find the way to acquire it through
inner work upon ourselves. You see, we have entered the age of the
consciousness soul, leaving behind us the age of the rational or mind
soul which informed the Graeco-Roman era. And this consciousness
soul must increasingly develop in such a way that the beings of the
higher hierarchies no longer work into us, for this would darken our
awareness, but instead we must consciously elevate ourselves to
them. Our fully aware, bright, clear day consciousness will be
composed of this effort of self-elevation to the higher hierarchies.
Spiritual science is the beginning of these endeavours. It does not
originate in anything arbitrary but arises from insight into the radical
changes at work in our time.

But there are various other things too that we must consciously
develop. Humankind has always had to live according to the laws of
karma, the great laws of destiny, but has not always been aware of
these. Lessing's *Education of the Human Race*[46] took the world by
surprise when it appeared, as if fully formed, from modern culture,
and brought with it an awareness of repeated lives on earth. The time
is now beginning when we cannot any longer interact and live with
each other as in past eras. We have already seen that we cannot have
the same relationship as we once did to the three higher hierarchies,
but the same is true of our relationships with other human beings.
The life humankind once led continues to influence us today, but we
neglect our duties to the modern age if we do not emphasize the need
for a new form of relationship between people. So far this did not
matter since human consciousness was not obliged to take itself in

hand in the past, and in former times people related to each other without knowing that a soul lives within us which, before its latest birth, lived another life on earth. A time will come, and is dawning already, when it would be an inner flaw in us to be ignorant of something living in another person's soul that originates in a former life on earth. Until now it did not matter that people were unaware of this. But now a time begins when it should not be ignored. Let me illustrate this with an example.

Among the social impulses we sought to develop was a school founded in a really new human spirit—the Waldorf school affiliated for the time being with the Waldorf-Astoria cigarette factory. Last Sunday we celebrated its opening,[47] preceded by a seminar that I gave for teachers.[48] Here the primary emphasis was on founding a pedagogy, an art of education and teaching, which takes full account that within the child is developing a soul originating in a former life on earth. Hitherto teachers, even very 'progressive' ones, saw their task as developing certain emergent skills and capacities from the child's soul; and yet they could only see, more or less, what could be drawn forth from the body of the child. This will not be sufficient in future for fulfilling the teacher's profession. Instead, a teacher will have to have a fine sense of what is emerging in the growing child from former lives on earth, and this will be a radical change in the education of the future: using this insight to draw out of the child what needs to be developed. But before this can happen, social conditions must arise that are founded on our spiritual relationship with other people: an awareness that a resurrected soul, in a sense, is there before you in another human being and originates in a previous incarnation. It is not enough to possess this as theoretical knowledge only, a kind of conceptual world-view, but it must also become practical—so much so that it forms the sound basis for an art of education, an art of teaching.

That is what makes this approach a living and life-enhancing one. And it is therefore self-evident that there is as yet little receptivity for such things and that people look askance at those with a spiritual outlook who perceive what is needed today. What is needed, rather than the trumpeting of certain spiritual world-views, is to cast the sunlight of knowledge upon specific and tangible areas of life. It is not about formulaic utterances but about implementing such knowledge in the very life of humanity. In founding a new pedagogy we discern very clearly how the past, with its empty phrases, collides with a new age.

I have taken pains to inform myself thoroughly about modern educational approaches. Often—I will give only one example here—people ask whether the form or content of education is more important. Should we educate people with certain professions in view, so that they find their proper place in civil life, or should we pay more attention to human nature itself, drawing out of children more generally human attributes in a humanistic approach? There has been much debate about this in educational circles. But this is only phrase-mongering since there is such divergence here between what people say and any inwardly comprehended truth. Are people anything other than the conditions they grow into? Take modern civil servants as an example. By what means are they dedicated to public office? By the fact that past generations established this or that institution. Public life today is only the outcome of what earlier generations created. Is this why teachers of the past focused on the content of education rather than the manner of delivering it? It is true that they did so, and yet the two approaches are one and the same! And so the debates that rage are about things that amount to the same thing. Something else is important: that in the children born today we find the tendencies and inclinations that will develop and mature in the next generation and the one after that—that in other words we are educating for the future. Whether we teach people with an emphasis on content or form, the latter being seen as 'humanistic', is mere phrase. But that we must educate for the future, must predict and prefigure the tasks of coming generations, is a serious and important matter and intrinsic to the life of the world.

People today say such things are hard to grasp, but they will have to get used to grasping them since otherwise, increasingly, modern developments will leave them stranded. This is really extremely important. We have to become more aware, in the fullest and most serious sense, both because we must find a connection with the work of the beings of the higher hierarchies, and also because a new kind of relationship is necessary between people themselves in the field of education. In every person who stands before us, every child, we must nurture not just the present soul but the one who has emerged from former conditions on earth. This is something we must remain continually aware of. It is so important that we find a real, tangible relationship to the spirit. Just knowing something about karma, about recurring lives on earth, about the human constitution, is fine as theoretical knowledge, as a world-view, but this will not get us very far in itself. Only when this theoretical world-view comes alive does it become what humanity needs in the immediate future.

To these two truths, about our relationship to the higher hierarchies and about karma, we can add a third. From my account in *Knowledge of the Higher Worlds* you will know that when a person comes to perceive the world of spirit he inevitably has an experience referred to as the crossing of the threshold. I described this crossing of the threshold in terms of the three human soul faculties, which in physical life interact in a fairly chaotic manner, separating and becoming autonomous: the power of thinking, feeling and will. As a person crosses the threshold, these powers become independent of each other.

In many respects, the whole course of humanity's evolution resembles the life of an individual human being, although things are transposed. What we undergo consciously when we seek to perceive in the world of spirit, the so-called crossing of the threshold, is something that all humanity has to pass through during this fifth post-Atlantean epoch. There is no choice about this: humankind is passing through this experience unconsciously. Not the individual but all humanity, and each individual with humanity. What does this mean?

In future, our thinking, feeling and will that presently interact and work together in us will become sundered, and this is already becoming apparent in various domains. Humanity is in the process of passing unconsciously through a significant doorway that is clearly perceived by the seer. In this transition over the threshold, the realms of thinking, feeling and will diverge; but this obliges us to shape external life in a way that allows the human being to undergo this radical inner change in his outward life as well. As thinking in the life of humankind becomes more autonomous, we must establish a foundation on which it can unfold and develop in a sounder way, and the same is true for feeling and for will. The chaotically interwoven fabric of public life as it has been until now must be divided into three spheres: economic life; the life of rights or the political state; and cultural or spiritual life. This demand for social threefolding is connected with the secret of humanity's evolution in our era.

Please do not think that this threefold social organism is an arbitrary invention. It is born from the most intimate perception of humanity's evolution, and from what must happen if the aims of this evolution are not to be thwarted. We have suffered the terrible catastrophe of the world war in recent years because people found it so hard to discern a goal of a spiritual nature, and were so far removed from even acknowledging that such goals exist. We must now work our way out of such chaos, as the very course of humanity's evolution itself dictates. However, it seems to me that the need for social threefolding will only be thoroughly understood on an anthroposophic basis, through feeling and awareness of what is actually happening in our evolution. In our day people dislike acknowledging such things. They much prefer dealing with immediate, short-term issues rather than delving into the deeper secrets of existence.

Someone who gazes into these secrets is much saddened by this, finding humanity so completely disinclined to engage with what is most needed. But there is much more to be said. All pessimism is wrong. This does not mean that all optimism is right either, of course, but appealing to the will is certainly right. We should will and seek to realize what accords with humanity's rightful evolution, and in doing so we have to remind ourselves continually that the old era is past and we must draw a line under it. We can only gain true insights today if we draw a line under a past age, and can only count on a new era by making a spiritual reckoning. We should not deceive ourselves that we can carry forward into the new era what we have become so comfortable and familiar with in a past one, but instead must begin to turn to effective new ideas in outward life. Humanity stands at a crossroads. One path leads through mechanization of the mind and spirit, which has become very mechanical in modern times, especially in abstract laws of nature—which have then also been applied wholesale to the life of society. Mechanization of the spirit means a vegetating soul. Vegetables sleep, and the human soul also inclines to sleep—people are sleepwalking through the most important events.

It is true to say, indeed, that people have slept through the most important events of recent years, and they continue to do so now.

Standing where I do today, I want to say this: that the people of central Europe have allowed leading figures to speak untruths to them day after day, and are continuing in this blindness without being aware of it. People see that the Mark has fallen on the currency exchange to 2.15 centimes, but I haven't yet found a single person who understands the relationship between the falling currency market and other events of pressing importance. A word of three syllables—I won't tell you what it is right now—will give you the answer to why the value of the Mark is falling. But souls love to sleep, love to sleep so much that we allowed a great disappointment to come over us in central Europe, one to which, as you might say, people were looking forward beforehand. It was thought that when women get the vote in parliamentary elections things will be twice as reasonable as before. But then came the national assembly and we found that this doubling of common sense compared to the old German parliament was nowhere in evidence. Instead the old parties continued, perpetuated old ways, at a time when these parties should have vanished lock, stock and barrel. People have no clue what this means since souls are sleeping. Mechanization of the spirit—vegetation of souls!

And if we look eastwards we see a very marked increase in the animalization of bodies. Just as Americanization of the spirit is tantamount to mechanization of culture, so the Bolshevism spreading in the East reveals an animalization of bodies. These people criticize this or that, condemn it, out of their emotions, but they do not seek to grasp life's reality. And so humanity today faces a choice: either to move towards a mechanization of the mind and spirit, the vegetation of souls, the animalization of bodies or, on the other hand, to try to find the path towards an awakening of the spirit, to find it in impulses that accord with the age of the consciousness soul and connect the human soul to the work and activity of the higher hierarchies. They can seek to acknowledge that the conscious human soul originates in former lives on earth, and that a threefold society is needed. These things belong together. And those who unite in the movement we call anthroposophic spiritual science should feel themselves to be a core, a kernel, from which emanates the strength for social renewal. True social reform can only emerge from spiritual impulses, and for this reason we could have expected the best understanding for our social circumstances and conditions to come from those who belong to this movement.

Here then, in these new premises, we have spoken of some of the factors at work in modern life, along with pressing needs. I would like to think that this festive occasion will extend to an ongoing awareness, whenever we meet here, of these truths that are so vital to human evolution. The more we inform our anthroposophic work with such awareness, the more of a festive, sacred hue we lend to this work. And these premises will best be inaugurated through feelings we summon from such sources.

LECTURE 7

It should be apparent to you from yesterday evening's reflections how necessary it is for us nowadays to turn our inner eye towards spiritual-scientific insights, to the spheres of existence, the reality, in which the sway of the spirit within human evolution is clearly perceptible to those able to survey these regions of reality.

Since the mid-fifteenth century—as I told you—civilized humanity lives in a period when the human soul's former relationship to the superordinate beings of the three next higher hierarchies, the Angeloi, Archangeloi and Archai, will become completely different to what it used to be. Previously this relationship was one in which the beings of these three hierarchies worked upon humanity's evolution, furthering it out of their own interest and impulses. Now, however, we live in an era when the work of these beings of the higher hierarchies has concluded. These beings have no interest in continuing the work upon humanity's evolution which they previously accomplished. They will only form a new relationship with humankind in so far as human beings begin to engage with worlds of spirit out of free will, free intention. If in the forthcoming times human beings were not to do this, they would lose their connection with spiritual worlds since the beings of spiritual realms who belong to us have no intrinsic interest in us any longer. We will only awaken their interest if we concern ourselves with the world of spirit through our own inner impulse—or in other words, cultivate thoughts, feelings and impulses of will into which spiritual powers can flow.

But now you can ask this question, and should do so in fact in relation to yesterday's reflections: by what means initially do we concern ourselves with worlds of spirit so that in the future, as we evolve on earth, we can maintain our relationship with these higher hierarchies? Here I need to say things that may seem to have no immediate connection with this question. However, we will see that they create the foundation in the present for renewing and recreating our connections with the world of spirit in future. The first thing we must consider here is the efficacy of the various confessions, various religious outlooks and faiths that exist in civilization. Hitherto these confessions directed human hearts and souls towards the spiritual world in certain inevitable ways. In future, by contrast, they will either have to endeavour to allow something quite new to enter or otherwise they will increasingly serve to reinforce humankind's separation from the spiritual world. Today religious faiths and confessions are basically founded on and oriented to human egotism, as we can see by reflecting on a key theme and tenet of faith, that of the immortality of the human soul. By the way religious confessions usually handle this question we can see that they count greatly on egoistic human impulses. Mostly, when speaking of the soul's immortality, they are referring—albeit for deeper reasons that we will not discuss today—to the soul's continuing existence after death, the continuation of a life of soul. It is fairly easy to speak to people about this, since it offers wide scope for human egoism. People simply cannot endure the thought—quite irrespective of the truth—of not living on in some way after death. When we speak of life after death we always therefore encounter a degree of acknowledgement and understanding in the human soul. You can be certain that interest in the question of immortality, as this is usually discussed today, is egoistic. People do not wish to contemplate the death of the soul. Naturally any future-oriented world-view must speak of the soul's immortality, for, as you all know from anthroposophic spiritual science, this is a truth and reality. But religious faiths and confessions have not begun yet to accept the way in which anthroposophically oriented spiritual science speaks of the continuing existence of the soul after a person has physically died.

But something else is also important: that modern human beings hear immortality spoken of in a quite different way from accustomed views. Besides speaking of life after death when discussing the soul's immortality, we must speak also, and in relation to it, of this life here in the physical world between birth and death, and of the fact that, as you know, this life is a continuation too of the existence we led between our last death and the birth that brought us into physical existence again. Humanity will need to learn to see this physical life of ours between birth and death as the continuation of a spiritual existence prior to birth or conception. In every growing child, from day to day, from week to week and from year to year, we must perceive powers emerging from within that originate in worlds of spirit, which pass through birth and work upon the gradual elaboration of the human being from birth onwards into a person's later years. In a sense we will have to decipher the divine within the human being by intervening developmentally in the child's life. Social relations between people will need to integrate something of a religious impulse that permeates all our interpersonal connections. But the most essential thing will be that people become able to gain a feeling apprehension that this physical life of ours is a continuation of a spiritual life before birth, of soul-spiritual existence, rather than continually forgetting this.

Many other things connect with this, such as that we come to see again that our intrinsic human nature rests in the depths of our being and gradually emerges. On a previous occasion I described to you conditions prevailing in ancient times, earlier periods of evolution,[49] for example in the second post-Atlantean epoch as anthroposophy refers to it. I pointed out to you that back then human beings remained capable of development into old age in a way that is now available only to a very young person. Early in life we pass through a stage of physical development around the age of seven, at second dentition, and then a further metamorphosis, expressed in physical life, at puberty. After this, developments continue but proceed in a less noticeably outward way. It was not so in ancient times. Then, whatever soul-spiritual developments a person passed through came to expression at much later ages. Today we are already old at 16 or 18, and one finds to one's alarm that very young people appear old. Here's an example. Some time ago in Stuttgart the Cultural Committee met to discuss modern educational approaches.[50] All sorts of points of view were aired. Then a young man stood up—well, let's say a young man but I might also say an elderly youth, who said that he wishes to instruct society in the real ideals underlying education. He first uttered some very formulaic phrases, then read out a programme for the place of education in modern society. But he was continually interrupted, so much so that he had to finish his speech, and did this with these words: 'I see that age no longer understands its own youth.' Then he sat down again. I replied to his comment that I understood people's failure to comprehend what he was saying, but not for the reason he had given. In fact he was speaking from a far too aged perspective, like an old man. He had offered principles that were really abstract in the extreme, an attribute of old age. Usually people nowadays only develop up to a certain age, during which they absorb all sorts of things and are not ashamed of changing and developing. But then, some time in their twenties, they start being ashamed of changing and developing any further. It is a very rare thing today that people with grey hair and lined faces still look forward to the arrival of each new year because it will give their organism new developmental opportunities, will enable them to learn something new that they could not learn before because their organism was not yet ready for it. Nowadays people do not let their organism develop; they are ashamed to go on learning, to remain capable of development once they reach the youthful age of 30 or so. It would be important for a person to retain the capacity throughout life to look forward to each new year because each year conjured forth anew and differently the divine, spiritual contents of his inner being. This is something we must really learn: not just to change and develop when young but to experience ourselves as capable of development throughout our lives between birth and death. Naturally this will require a new form of education. When old people today think back to their schooldays this is not usually a pleasant memory. We must come to shape schooling so that when we recall it later in life we find in it a continually renewed source of vitality. You can see from this that here too we can find the means to really perceive the divine spirit within us, to experience in ourselves something above and beyond a life arising in us merely through external stimulus.

Other things too must be acknowledged today. People are as yet unaware of a secret of life intimately connected with our present evolutionary moment. In older times, before the mid-fifteenth century, there was no need to pay much attention to this secret, but today we must do so. It is this. As we are presently constituted, in body, soul and spirit, each night in a certain way we perceive the events of the coming day, albeit without these events coming to full, waking consciousness. It is our angel who has this prevision. In other words, what we experience during the night in community with the being we call our angel is a preview of the coming day. This is not said to awaken mere human curiosity—that would be quite mistaken—but for practical reasons, to enrich practical life. Only when we are inwardly pervaded by this knowledge and outlook will we make decisions in the right way, will we draw thoughts from the night and bring them properly to bear on the course of our day. Let us assume, in very specific terms, that a person is meant to do a particular thing at midday. His angel and he have already spoken together in the night of what he is to do then. This has been true for people since the mid-fifteenth century. We do not have to be aware of it, and it is not a subject for mere curiosity. But we ought to be pervaded by a sense that what we discuss with our angel in the preceding night should be made fruitful by us during the following day.

Much today of a shattering and shocking nature can point us towards what I have just said. These years of pain we have experienced, the past four or five years, can also very gradually teach humanity that there has been a lack of awareness of our connection with higher beings, a connection present in us each day through our experiences of the previous night. So much would have happened differently in these past four or five years if people had been pervaded by the sense of acting in harmony with the speech they had with their angel the night before. Today we must bring such things to light. People need to realize that this life between birth and death is a continuation of the life of soul and spirit we experienced before birth. We must speak of the importance of people experiencing the revelations of the divine in their being throughout their lives, and of bearing through waking life a strong sense that what they do from morning to evening is something that has been discussed during sleep with their angel.

We must turn to feelings of this kind, much more tangible feelings in relation to the world of spirit than the more abstract doctrines of religious confessions, and at the same time appeal not to egoistic but unegoistic impulses in human nature. Such feelings will give rise to the kind of relationship we need today with beings belonging to the hierarchy of angels. Then these beings will show interest in humankind again. Our sense of the world of spirit must move in this direction.

But there is something more. As you know, modern faiths speak a great deal about God and the divine, but what are they really speaking of when they do? Naturally they are speaking only of something of which at least a nascent awareness exists in the human soul. What matters is not the name you give something but what is present in the human soul. People speak of God, of Christ, but in fact they are frequently only speaking of their angel since this is what they can turn to, having an affinity with it in their souls. Irrespective of the doctrines of different faiths, of whether they speak of God or Christ or anything else, the thought substance out of which they speak always only encompasses the angelic beings belonging to humankind, the Angeloi. They do not reach higher than this first order of angelic beings since people today are disinclined to seek a relationship with the world of spirit founded on more than egoism. A connection with the Archangeloi, the hierarchy of Archangels, must be sought in a different way by substantially widening human interests so that people's feelings can ascend from an inclination to the Angeloi and reach as far as the Archangeloi.

People must have roughly the following inner experience, saying to themselves: in the past four or five years we have experienced terrible events across the civilized world. Many have wondered what the real cause of these events was, and many have laid the blame at each other's door. There has been much talk of guilt and innocence. And yet, if we look deeper than the most superficial of veneers we will have no interest in this talk of 'causes and origins', of guilt and innocence—simply because it will be apparent that what has risen to the surface of life over these recent years is like a wave brought to the surface of the ocean by the powers at work in its depths. As year succeeded year, the powers at work in the depths of humanity grew ever more turbulent. One nation after another participated in the great human idiocy of these past years, and all one can say is that elemental forces were swirling towards the surface. The ocean of human life had grown turbulent and restless. But for what reason?

We will not gain any clarity about this turbulence without seeing it as a really new development in human history. People will have to acknowledge that the battle that has raged over recent years is only the start of events which will unfold in a quite different domain but which have never before been seen in humanity. This is not the end but the beginning of the greatest conflicts, spiritual conflicts, in civilization, and a superficial reflection on human evolution can show this to be the case. It will take all our efforts and concern to be equal to these conflicts. In the forthcoming period East and West will increasingly be at risk of inner opposition and conflict since each has developed in a different direction. If we wish to understand these things, we will need to try to fathom some of the deep riddles of current phenomena.

For decades now, Marxist circles have been saying that art, religion, morals, law, science and so forth are all a kind of ideology. I spoke of this in more detail in *Towards Social Renewal*. In other words, the view of life that has developed amongst the ruling classes of civil society over the past three to four hundred years is one that these bourgeois circles have, in a rather cowardly way, not fully admitted or acknowledged, whereas socialist groups of the past half century have faced this head-on. They have said this: the real life of society consists only in what is actually happening in it—the commercial factors and powers of the economy. This alone is real. All that humanity elaborates as art, religion, ethics, as science, law and morality is just a kind of steam rising from this underlying reality. It is all mere ideology and has no intrinsic reality, just apparent reality. This relates in turn to the endeavours of socialist parties in the modern era, to their belief that they need only change economic life and then everything else in society will change. Everything else, morals, ethics, law, religion and so forth is, they say, a kind of hot air, an unreality rising as ideology from the only true reality of economic life.

But if we broaden our view of things from such a narrow focus we will take issue with this view of 'ideology', which the ruling classes too could have held for the past three to four hundred years if they had not been too cowardly to do so. They too have felt that economic life is the only reality and that science, art, religion and so forth rise from this reality like steam. This was the underlying view of life, and the socialists, as its students, have merely drawn the final conclusions from it. The socialists have simply studied this bourgeois world and taken the same perceptions to an extreme. But what I have now expressed is the view that developed in the West, culminating there in the second half of the nineteenth century, and in the twentieth.

Other impulses in the Orient have led to a world-view that states, by contrast: 'I look upon what occurs outwardly in the world. I see the impressions my senses mediate; I see what I use as tools to work on the world and change it, and on what shines down to me from the stars. I look too upon my own bodily form. What is this all? It is maya, or illusion. The nature of true reality by contrast is what I experience within my soul.' If we translate this word 'maya'—not by looking it up in a dictionary but by pondering its meaning inwardly—we find that it actually equates with the word 'ideology' in the West. For millennia people in the East have regarded the outer world that acts upon our senses, including the economy, as maya. In the West on the other hand people regard as reality what orientals think of as maya or illusion, and see all that rises within the soul as ideology. Both views of the world have attained a certain level. If you ask the leaders of socialist parties, especially in regions where the first revolution—along the lines of the 'November revolution'[51]—has not yet occurred, they will still tell you the same thing that people were saying until the Great War broke out: that transformation, revolutionizing of the world does not require any active will but that it will come about by itself. The November revolution did alter the ideas of socialist leaders to some extent—not their feelings but their ideas and concepts. In this view that nothing much needed to be done, that things would change by themselves, we encounter a fatalistic element that made headway in the West. People said that one need only wait for the means of production to develop to the stage where private capital, and everything concentrated in it, would alter by itself into other forms. This was like saying that the air in this room is stale and I can no longer breathe. I could open the window but I do not do so. Instead I'll wait for the air to improve by itself.

Fatalism in the West, fatalism in the East: we know these well. In the Orient, as the world-view of maya evolved, people eventually succumbed to complete fatalism. Every world-view has the seeds of fatalism within it. But today we have reached a point when we must emerge from such fatalism. A transition must be found from mere passive observation to the will. To fire our will we must find impulses such as those I have offered: to see our birth as a continuation of pre-birth life; to remain young at heart even when our hair grows white and our faces lined; to acknowledge the nightly work of the angels and how this plays into our daily lives. This is what is needed. It is necessary that we absorb such impulses into our will, thus broadening our scope of interest rather than focusing narrowly on what only affects our own private, individual lives. We must gain a sense of the divergences between East and West. The inner world we in the

West see as 'ideology' and the outer world we see as 'reality'. In the East it is the opposite: there the outer world is 'maya' or illusion, and the inner world is reality. Faced with this collision between East and West in the modern world, we need to invoke our will in order to emerge from what has become fatalism in these world-views. We must seek this path but will only find it if we can subscribe seriously to something that the rest of humanity still finds terribly irritating.

On one occasion, in a lecture in a city in southern Germany,[52] I said something that greatly irritated people but which elicited a curious echo. I had uttered one of the truths that must be spoken today. It is not possible to frame the things one speaks in a way that people like. The truth must be spoken. In the context of my lecture, I said that the ruling classes of today have a decadent physical brain. As well as being disagreeable to hear this, it is also an unpleasant thing to say, and yet it is necessary for people to hear it. Specifically those who have shaped the times we now live in possess a decadent physical brain. This is simply a fact. Today in some respects we are in a similar situation to the people of Europe at the time of the Migration Period and the spread of Christianity. From the Orient came the Christian impulse, passing first through Greece and Rome. The Greek and Roman world was of course more highly developed than the Teutonic. The Teutons were barbarians. Yet the brains of the Greeks and the Romans were decadent, and for this reason the wave of Christianity was not taken up and absorbed by them in the way it was when the Germans encountered it. This was the horizontal Migration Period. Today it is vertical: a wave of spiritual life descending from the world of spirit. Just as Christianity first surged over the Greeks and Romans so now the world of spirit is surging over the modern world, over middle-class society, and the latter is decadent. The proletariat however is not yet decadent; the working classes can still comprehend what is meant by the world of spirit. But the others will need the preparation that anthroposophy affords; in other words, they will have to develop the part of the brain that is not yet physical, the etheric brain. Today, inevitably, the ruling classes of society will soon not only possess a decadent brain but will become entirely decadent if they fail to understand that they must employ supersensible means to comprehend a spiritual world-view.

That is the tragedy of the intellectual middle classes; they wish to comprehend everything in physical terms whereas today we must grasp things with the etheric brain—that is, absorb spiritual truths. This is the direction modern humanity must advance in, and here the West must take the lead. And in this regard we have to recognize something very important.

If you study philology, the development of language across the globe, and in particular examine the German language, you will find that it is subject today to terrible misuse. Yet we know, if we look back a little way to the language of Goethe or Lessing, that not so long ago words in German were capable of according with spiritual reality, of giving apt expression to it. Nowadays we have neglected language terribly, devalued it to empty phrases. As yet language itself has not become so devalued that it cannot be spiritual. But the further West we go, to western languages, the more we find that these languages themselves are increasingly devoid of the real spiritual element—that they have discarded spirit from their sounds and very tone, even from their grammatical constructions. This discarding of soul and spirit from Anglo-American idiom leads to the global mission of these peoples. Their world mission consists in learning as they listen to others—they learn this quite instinctively, but they learn it as they seize world dominion—not only to hear tone and speech sound but also to interpret the gesture of language: to hear, more than the merely physical speech sound, something that passes between people as they speak and yet also goes beyond what is spoken. This is something that passes between their etheric bodies. The secret of western languages is that the physical tone as such is losing its importance while the spiritual element gains in importance. It is part and parcel of these people's task to let spirit infuse language: not only to hear physically but to intuit, to feel and sense more than is actually contained in the sounds of speech. In the West, therefore, it will be necessary to seek the spirit through language itself.

If we look to the East, by contrast, we discover an increasing urge in oriental people, as they engage in inner contemplation, not to make do with the ideas of karma and reincarnation developed in earlier times but to go beyond this and look out into the world, there hearkening to spirit and also founding a kind of vision of nature.

These are just small examples of ways to broaden our interests, going beyond our own personal domain and, from the perspective of our own national characteristics, gaining a view of the whole of humanity. We can look westwards and see ideology at work there, though of a different kind from that in the East. But at the same time we see how these contrasts give rise to a turbulence of elemental power that is stirred up within humanity. We learn to perceive our place within the whole civilized world; and developing such perception, we can also invoke in ourselves feelings by means of which we can ascend to the sphere of the Angeloi. The scope of our interests is simply broadened to such an extent that we become inclined to concepts that rise to the sphere of the Archangeloi. You see, everything I have told you now about the contrast between ideology and maya and so forth is something whose primal powers unfold in the sphere of the Archangeloi, the Archangels. Here we pass beyond the sphere of the Angeloi. And from this you can see what modern humanity really needs. If someone speaks as I have done now about maya and ideology and so forth, and even of the primal powers in the sphere of the Archangeloi in which these powers originate, clever folk will think him a half-wit. This is because the mentality, the intellectual acuity people have achieved has closed them off from the great interests of humanity. We can only broaden the scope of our interests from a spiritual perspective, by penetrating the sphere where work unfolds in relation to matters of great concern for humanity.

Now I have given you an idea of how we can work our way upwards into the sphere of the Archangeloi. We can work our way up still higher, and this is also something that modern humankind must learn. Our educated classes have been compelled to look back to Greek times. That is, in so far as they were men—though the same thing now holds true for the education of young women—they had to have a grammar school education during which they absorbed aspects of ancient Greek culture. This enabled them increasingly to feel their way back into the world of ancient Greece, motivated them to do so. This is highly significant for our civilization: that in our most formative years, we learn what the Greeks achieved. The Greeks themselves did things differently—it did not of course occur to them to make their youngsters learn Egyptian, but instead they attended to their own immediate reality. The Greeks had a sense for immediate reality, whereas we occupy our young people with anything other than the reality of their surroundings. We do not give them an inclination for reality but transpose them back into ancient times. And we have no idea at all what we are doing in the process. You see, we are not just teaching young ladies and gentlemen ancient Greek language but also something that lies in the very sounds and grammar of that language: the whole character of a nation and people. By absorbing ancient Greek, as is the practice today, a person's soul also assumes a configuration resembling the ancient Greek disposition. Ancient Greek culture allowed only a small stratum of society to participate in culture, while all others were slaves. In Greece only a free man was permitted to engage with science, politics and, at the most—but only under supervision—with agriculture, whereas everything else was performed by slaves. And this fact is embedded in the language itself. By appropriating ancient Greek culture and language, we are uniting our own culture with an aristocratic outlook. It was natural for the Greeks to orient their whole social organism to this culture, for the latter was connected with the blood, with the line of descent. There were the broad masses, and then those of a higher stratum, who possessed a higher life of culture already by virtue of their blood.

This comes to expression even in Greek sculpture. Compare the Mercury type with the Zeus or Athene type: a different position of nose and ears. The Greek knew exactly what he was trying to express in his distinction between the Mercury type on the one hand and the Zeus type on the other.

All this still influences us far more than we realize. As we form our world-views today we are in fact still formulating ideas born from outlooks in ancient Greece based on blood descent. Our culture is pervaded by what we absorb from ancient Greece; it intrudes into our era in a luciferic fashion. Greek culture metamorphosed into Roman culture and was succeeded by it. Compared to the Greeks, the Romans were a down-to-earth, prosaic people, and developed other aspects of life. What Greek culture based on bloodline the Romans embodied in more abstract form as 'citizen of the state'. In Roman times a person was not so much a human being as a citizen. This would have been incomprehensible to the Greeks: that one is not what one is by virtue of being human but by having one's existence registered in a state archive. This can sometimes assume grotesque forms. I once had a friend who was old—he was 64. One day he said to me: 'I have now saved enough money'—he had always been poor as a church mouse—'to marry the love of my youth.' He had got engaged at 18, but at the time did not have enough money to marry. The two swore to wait for each other until they could marry, and this had finally become possible. By now he was 64 and she was 62. So he returned home and wrote to tell her they could marry at last since he had enough money. But they still could not get married because his parish doubted his existence. The rectory, you see, had burned down many years before, and all birth certificates with it, and there was no one left who could confirm who he was. He himself thought that the fact he was standing there ought to be proof enough, yet there was no legal proof! Eventually they did succeed in getting married, but these difficulties brought home to him how much more important a certificate was than an actual person.

In other words, one is a citizen: one is what one is in an abstract context. This outlook is essentially Roman, and everything of this kind that exists in ordinary life is essentially Roman too. Our education is largely taken in hand by the state, which has become so abstract, and which will become a great deal more so still as socialism's influence is increasingly felt. Nowadays people are not educated so as to take their place in the world as human beings but for a civil profession—adapted to the needs of such work. The state takes young people in hand—well, not immediately, since to begin with they are still too bothersome. It leaves them to parents for a while. But then it extends its claws, gets hold of them and trains them to be what it requires. And it knows very well that people will serve its needs, since it gives them so much, doesn't it? It gives them an economic life, everything they are entitled to, and then pensions them off afterwards. You can hear what it means to people to be able to say that they not only get paid for their work but afterwards even get a pension! This is something very pervasive and chains people to the abstract state—and then also pervades their whole outlook. Here too the Roman outlook informs people. People today will not understand you if you tell them that they must kindle and activate something in their soul to have a share in their own immortality, to be able to carry their soul actively through the gate of death. They have become entirely unaccustomed to comprehending such a thing. Instead they are told they need only believe in Christ and in whatever the state does. And they see that they are first provided for by the state, and, once they have worked enough, are pensioned off by it. The Church takes this one step further; after death it pensions off the human soul so that a person does not actually have to work upon his soul during his lifetime nor do anything to carry it through the gate of death afterwards. Nowadays people are registered and catered for: this Roman state is the second thing we have increasingly absorbed into ourselves.

You can discover dire things in this realm. I have just come back from Stuttgart where I was helping set up the Waldorf School, and for this purpose I had to examine various curriculum plans. If I think back to the 70s and 80s of the last century, curricula were fairly short; they just contained the content of subjects that should be taught in each class—learning objectives and content. Otherwise and in every other respect, teachers were free. But now you find very extensive curricula, in which it is officially decreed exactly how you are meant to teach a subject. Thus the effect of a living individual on another living individual—which is the only thing that matters—is now enshrined in laws and ordinances, has become subject to official decree. This means the death of spiritual life; and this death leads straight back from central Europe to ancient Rome. So the second thing we have absorbed and integrated is this political, legal state, originating in Roman culture.

In addition to this is something that cannot be transplanted from ancient times into modern ones—economic life. You see, we can regurgitate what the Greeks perceived and knew, can allow the legislative life of the Roman state to impinge on us, but we cannot eat what the Greeks and Romans ate. Economic life has to be a modern affair. Gradually we have succeeded in mingling our economic life with Greek culture, with the Roman state. But now we have the task of separating these things from each other once more, of coming to see that these three strata of society that have coagulated in a sense from diverse eras, must now be sundered. This also means broadening the scope of our interests—as we did before towards both the Orient and the Occident in spatial, geographic terms—by bringing them into the present. In turn this means raising ourselves, making ourselves capable of feelings that can raise us to the Archai. But how many people today wish to develop an interest in these things: an unprejudiced interest in how the zeitgeist works as it interweaves different eras as I described it? In Stuttgart I spoke about the denatured form of our grammar school education.[53] I don't know if this was merely accidental but, a few days after my talk, big announcements appeared in the Stuttgart newspapers, signed by all kinds of important figures, professors and so on, stating that a grammar school education should not be undervalued, and that it had made fine contributions to the greatness of the German people which had come so gloriously to the fore in recent times. It is hard to credit, but this was literally what was said by the educators of our youth in April 1919, just a few months after October 1918. In our time such things are possible. Other things are possible too.

We cannot get any further until we come to see how we must absorb impulses that flow from the world of spirit into our physical world, understanding that just as we are connected through our corporeal organism with the animal kingdom, plant kingdom and mineral kingdom so our spiritual organization is connected with the hierarchies of the Angeloi, Archangeloi and Archai: spirits of personality as the guardians of personal development, nation spirits as the guardians of a people's ongoing development within spatial conditions, and time spirits as the guardians of evolution through time. We must grasp these in their spiritual foundations. Everything today depends on this: that we find the courage and strength to look into the world of spirit. We stand at the beginning of a surge of dire conflict, of great turmoil in all human instincts that arise from the half-truth, on the one hand, that economic life is the only reality and that all soul and spirit are ideology; and on the other that soul and spirit are the only reality and everything outward is merely maya. These contrary views will unleash in human nature instincts of a kind that will long, long feed the flames of spiritual battle, in forms of which humanity today as yet has no inkling. We need to know this; and we will need to know, also, how we can raise ourselves to vision of the world of spirit as the times require us to.

The times themselves command and prompt this, and we must attend to it. We will speak further of this tomorrow.

LECTURE 8

As I said, our current era in humanity's evolution is one that faces us with great trials even if a great part of what undergoes these trials unfolds in the subconscious depths of the human soul.

People know, and must know what it means to cross the threshold into the invisible world when they undergo a form of initiation and really do enter this invisible world. Yet something similar is also at work—though naturally not all at once but over longer spans of time—with the whole of humanity: the interwoven powers of thinking, feeling and will gradually become independent as humanity crosses the threshold into supersensible worlds. These powers will separate in a sense, will extricate themselves from each other in human experience. All this is connected with significant changes in our deepest human nature—changes which must begin to be integrated into our awareness. Yet today people are drawn instead towards the comfort of ignoring what is actually happening within humanity; they give themselves up to illusions, and mere dreams, really, about life. And this is a tendency we have to overcome.

What I wish to say to you today is something best comprehended if we recall realities of existence that have long been familiar to us: the departure of our I and astral nature from physical and etheric bodies when we fall asleep, and our return to them when we awaken. This is a general and in some respects schematic way of describing what happens. In general we can say that on awakening we re-enter our physical body and ether body, but in a sense this re-entry occurs to diverse degrees. If for instance we consider a young child, we can never say that his I and astral body completely immerse themselves in the physical and etheric bodies, and that their action is merged entirely with that of the physical and etheric. In a sense something of the I and astral body does not unite with the physical and etheric. And if we look back to earlier times of humanity's evolution—before that incisive turning point in our evolution which, as I said, lies in the middle of the fifteenth century—then we can see that until then the I and the astral body did not fully immerse themselves during waking life, during periods of waking consciousness. It is of huge evolutionary significance in our post-Atlantean era that our soul and spirit, our I and astral body, can now fully immerse themselves in our physical and etheric bodies. In our present times—and later on these circumstances will again change to some degree—this happens from around the age of 27 or 28. This is a very important secret of humanity's evolution. Only now, really, do we experience ourselves as fully inhabiting the physical body, and only when we reach the mature age of 27 or 28. What is the significance of this complete immersion in the physical body? By this means we become able to develop thoughts, unfold ideas, that embody materialistic science as it has come to the fore since the time of Galileo and Copernicus.[54] Our physical body is the right tool for these ideas, for this scientific view of the world. In former centuries this condition was not attained in waking life, and therefore scientific thinking in its present form did not exist. It is entirely bound up with the physical body; and this relates to everything I have been saying to you recently about the activity we must develop in terms of spiritual-scientific insights, so as to reawaken the interest of the three hierarchies of beings immediately above us, as I described them. These beings of the three hierarchies have brought us to the point of being able to immerse ourselves in our physical body, and thus acquaint ourselves scientifically with the dead mineral world of our external environment.

In our present times it is, quite simply, the task of humanity to know about such things. Without being aware of them, we are in a sense sleepwalking through our era, failing to perceive the real nature of events occurring around us. These tangible realities are ones we must allow to work upon our soul so that we become aware of the nature of forces currently holding sway in humanity's evolution. In our age—by which I mean of course a long span of time—much renewal is needed. Above all such things as the aims of education must find renewal, as I have suggested previously.[55] We have to educate people from childhood on so that at the age I indicated they become able to immerse themselves fully in the physical body. We must make it possible for this to happen. Our efforts to transform and renew education are needed in order to prepare people to experience and undergo a new stage of evolution. If we observe life we will know that there are many broken human beings today— people who cannot cope with life. Why can they not? It is because they are unable to look back to experiences they should have had in their schooldays, in their childhood. Certain powers can only be developed in childhood. If they are, they remain available through-out life as a possession which enables us to cope with what comes at us. If we do not have these powers, we can't cope with life, quite simply. Awareness of this can give us the real sense of responsibility we should have for education and the education system.

Another thing. We must be clear that the Christ impulse entered humanity in the fourth post-Atlantean epoch, which began in the eighth century BC and lasted until the middle of the fifteenth century of our era. Roughly after a third of this period had elapsed, the Christ impulse entered earthly evolution, the event of Golgotha, endowing it with its intrinsic meaning. This event occurred at the point when humanity was in the process of developing the rational or mind soul. This stage of evolution, during which human thinking and feeling was more instinctive than today, was followed by a stage, from the fifteenth century, during which the consciousness soul developed. That is the stage we still find ourselves in today. The way in which the event of Golgotha entered humanity as a world-historical impulse, was initially adapted to the instinctive understanding of the fourth post-Atlantean epoch, and was thus absorbed by the people of those times. It was quite natural for people with this kind of instinctive comprehension to think of the Christ being living within the individual Jesus of Nazareth, to conceive that this being had descended from cosmic heights in order to unite with the body of Jesus of Nazareth. Everyone was at that time able to recognize in the event of Golgotha a great, hugely significant supersensible occurrence entering humanity. But as time continued, this recognition increasingly faded as the powers at work in the rational or mind soul dimmed. Understanding of the event of Golgotha that still prevailed in the early Christian centuries could not endure but was superseded by a quite different inner state amongst civilized humanity. As the age of the consciousness soul dawned, the event of Golgotha itself was perceived in ever more material ways. Over the past four or five hundred years, therefore, as civilization has developed, understanding of what actually happened at Golgotha—the indwelling of Christ in Jesus of Nazareth—has continually diminished. This great mystery, instinctively perceived and acknowledged in the early Christian centuries, has receded ever further from the grasp of our understanding. It has become ever more materialized, to the point when, in our own day, people no longer give any credence to the supersensible, cosmic Christ—and this is regarded as progress. Instead people have begun to speak of Jesus of Nazareth as a person who, albeit extraordinary, was otherwise just like any other person.

Here too we find ourselves at a point of transition. A new understanding of Christ must dawn. This new understanding can only dawn, however, if it is sought with the means offered by spiritual science, with supersensible means which alone can discover something that, while manifesting in the sensory domain, could only in fact be accomplished in the supersensible realm. This new understanding of Christ must emerge from depths of human nature in which all religious divergences and disagreements that otherwise fracture humanity fall silent. These confessional differences are all rooted in a realm of the soul that is closer to the surface, more superficial, than everything which, drawn from deeper, underlying regions, must, through spiritual science, lead to a new understanding of the Christ within Jesus. And this understanding will not be complete, will not really satisfy the thirst of the modern human soul, if it does not at the same time bridge the divergences in humanity which the different confessions have bred. Of this new Christ impulse we may hope for something that we all must yearn for, really, if we think of humanity in a serious and worthy fashion. This is sought today in other domains, but with very little understanding. Nowadays people pin great hopes on a so-called League of Nations. It is curious how people today are drawn to abstractions as they seek to understand reality. Where should the impulses originate that can work within and between nations and connect them in a so-called League of Nations? Everything that has so far formed the basis of this League of Nations amounts to nothing but a few abstractions. But people are sleepwalking through such things, and we can see the degree to which they do so in a fact such as the following. Before America had involved itself in all the current global negotiations, Woodrow Wilson,[56] the inventor, or at least the re-inventor, of this League of Nations, stated that the League could only be properly founded through acknowledgement that there were no victors or vanquished in this catastrophic war. That, he said, would be the indispensible precondition for the League. Anyone who took this seriously at the time cannot possibly take seriously what is now being said about this League of Nations: the two things are irreconcilable. But people fail to see this. And the fact that people accept irreconcilably contradictory things once a little time has elapsed really militates against any healthy human progress. It is as if people today are not fully inwardly present in what is happening.

No, this League of Nations amounts to absolutely nothing. And this, you see, is because things that must be established in humanity must flow to the surface from the depths of human nature. Only a new recognition of the Christ impulse can develop in us something established through all civilized humanity that is not founded on the differences between nations, and only this accords with contemporary needs. This Christ impulse, comprehended in a new, spiritual-scientific way, is the only thing that can reunite different peoples fractured by hatred and misunderstanding. And this is something that must inscribe itself very deeply in our souls as strong conviction. Everything that tends in another direction will inhibit and obstruct humanity's evolution. Basically it is frivolous to speak of the needs of human evolution today in any other way than out of its deepest foundations. If the earth and humanity's evolution received its true meaning and purpose through the event of Golgotha, today the time has come when this meaning and purpose must be grasped again in a new way. Unless humankind feels obliged to develop such understanding, no healing will come for the wounds of our age. The things that have to happen today cannot be seen separately from each other but belong together. You can't 'do' politics externally, you can't just set up an outward League of Nations. These things must be internalized through the Christ impulse, the deepest impulse at work in humanity.

Anthroposophically oriented spiritual science is obliged to focus on what every person can and must activate within himself simply as a single individual. You see, the moment we touch on these things, we must feel the whole seriousness of our age. It is profoundly painful to experience how little sense there is of the gravity of our times, that people avoid approaching insights of great scope and importance which very definitely must be integrated into human awareness. We have passed through an era that has greatly diverted us away from the inner motivation that can lead us to the insights we need today. If you ask a modern scientist or someone whose thinking runs along modern scientific lines what would have happened in earth evolution if the human being had not been a participant in it, he will inevitably tell you, if he draws the necessary conclusions from his views and hypotheses, that the earth would have simply evolved without us, would have evolved its mineral, plant and animal kingdoms irrespective of our absence. In his view the earth would evolve more or less as it has done in the absence of the human being, and there would therefore of course be no houses, cities and suchlike. If we take the modern scientific perspective we inevitably assume that the earth would have evolved without the human being. And yet this is entirely erroneous. If you survey all that we have discussed on various occasions over almost two years now, you will feel that what I now have to say is self-evident; and yet our attention does still need to be drawn to it.

The physical body we bear with us is interwoven with a soul element during our existence between birth and death. Now we have entered the current epoch, in fact, it is permeated by the soul in a particular way: the I and the astral body immerse themselves fully in the physical body. And whether our physical corpse is assigned to fire at cremation or to the earth through burial, modern science sees this merely as the diverse substances that composed this body returning to the earth at death in accordance with principles we can study in organic and particularly inorganic chemistry. But all this is nonsense. The truth rather is this: that the body we inhabit from birth to death is far from untouched by the human being's soul and spirit, which leave their imprint in the body. And we assign our corpse to the earth in a form and condition that it can only have acquired because it was inhabited from birth to death by the entelechy that lived as human soul-spirit in the world of spirit prior to our conception. The earth as it has evolved so far would long since have crumbled to dust, succumbed to aridity if it had not absorbed the leaven of human bodies—whether through burial or cremation—that have been enlivened until death by human souls. When people baked bread in the old days—nowadays this process has become a little more artificial—they kept back a little of the dough that was then used at the next baking as yeast or leaven. Similarly, the earth would not be able to evolve without human bodies—not animal ones—added to it as leaven. They ensure that the earth, which would otherwise long since have dried up and grown desiccated, can bear what it carries within it until the end of its evolution. In other words we participate in the whole of the earth's evolution, and do so even more at the present stage of our development. What passes to the earth's evolution when we die has significance for it.

In our present era and stage of evolution and on into the future, when we reach the age of maturity after 27 or 28, we are connected

with our physical body in waking life in a way that acts in a distinctive way upon the world of spirit, the supersensible world. This is
the remarkable polarity in human evolution: when we pass through
the portal of death, we leave our body behind and in doing so we
sunder from it something that serves the earth as the leaven of its
evolution. If we have reached the age of 28 through to 35, at death
we surrender to the world of spirit something that this world of spirit
needs. On a future occasion I will show how the state of affairs is
somewhat different for younger people who die before this age. That
would lead us too far today. But what we surrender in this way to the
world of spirit is the most important part of what we rediscover after
death when we re-experience our life in reverse in the world of spirit.

Secrets such as these are connected with humanity's evolution, and
should be absorbed and integrated into modern human awareness.
Such things are really nothing at all to do with curiosity and sen-
sationalism, but have a very, very different importance. If you can
take such things seriously, experiencing their full import within you,
then you can find a much more serious stance towards life than
others. And this deeper sense of life's seriousness is something that
modern people need. Full understanding of the aims of our threefold
social organism—as opposed to outward understanding which can
and must also be communicated to the outer or exoteric world—
must be founded on this sense of seriousness which draws upon
anthroposophically oriented spiritual science. This alone makes it
possible to participate in modern social evolution in the most conscious and intentional way. Otherwise we do not grasp things with
sufficient depth. Things connected with social threefolding must be
aired in public. But here, amongst ourselves, I hope we can kindle
sufficient fire, the necessary enthusiasm so that those who can
develop such understanding from a spiritual-scientific perspective
can do all in their power to impart this understanding to others
through the warmth of their own conviction, through their own
enthusiasm. The seriousness needed nowadays will not develop
through the superficial kinds of knowledge generally possessed by
people today, which leads to beliefs such as that the earth can evolve

perfectly well without the presence of the human being. And this is why, when we go through big cities today, our heart bleeds to witness the complete lack of real connection in people with what is actually unfolding in human evolution.

These things have been developing, and the catastrophic world war is a first culmination of the superficiality of outlook that increasingly holds sway. But our duty nowadays is to arrive at that threefold deepening I spoke of yesterday towards the beings of the three hierarchies above us. We have to recognize that we dwell in this context of realities. As humanity we must pass through an era in which the I and the astral body are descending most deeply into the physical and etheric bodies, and are therefore exposed to the greatest temptations, due to the fact that we enter into such close connection with our physical body.

There are two things to note here: firstly the way in which this temptation can manifest in what I will call its 'western' form, and secondly its 'eastern' one. The western form surfaces in ever more distinct ways as we turn our gaze towards the West, but it is a temptation which we bear very strongly in our own nature. Due to the fact that we are immersed ever more deeply in our physical body, we forge an intimate bond with the earthly forces with which the physical body is connected. Our physical body is bound up with earthly forces and can only detach itself from them by overcoming, in its awareness, the gravity of the earth and other such things that connect it to the earth. We have no idea of how we can overcome the forces at work in us through our organization. On one occasion here I referred to something that can illustrate what I mean. I said that the human brain is so heavy that if its whole weight came to effect it would crush the blood vessels immediately below it. But in fact our organism is so remarkably configured that this brain of ours floats in the cerebrospinal fluid. In line with the Archimedean principle, a body is lightened by an amount equal to the weight of the water it displaces. For this reason, the pressure of the brain on underlying blood vessels is reduced accordingly, because the brain floats in the cerebrospinal fluid and we can therefore overcome the brain's weight.

We overcome many things in this way. These forces, to which so little attention is paid, reveal that in the physical realm too the human organism testifies to cosmic wonders. We are connected with the forces of the earth but we must not become directly subject to them. The temptation to be too immediately bound up with them exists in the Occident, in all occidental feelings about life, and this temptation is an ahrimanic one. We can only counteract it in so far as we gradually succeed in deepening our insights to the point where we can survey the historical evolution of humanity and recognize, really understand, the Mystery of Golgotha as a reality occurring at the midpoint of this evolution. The occidental world-view can only be safeguarded against the ahrimanic temptation and its consequences if this world-view accepts the Christ into its cognitive reflections and quest for knowledge, if Christ can enter in to all western thinking.

The oriental world-view is in the opposite position. In some respects orientals retain a childlike perspective by holding back their I and astral body from fully descending into the physical and etheric body, even in the current age when humanity is destined to engage in this descent. The oriental flees this immersion. It is interesting to examine from this perspective some of the most salient phenomena of modern times. Rabindranath Tagore has given some very fine speeches, which have been translated into German and other languages.[57] If you read these, and have a sense for such things, you will discover that they have a quite different flavour from anything we find when we read western authors. A different spirit entirely. Just as oriental paintings and drawings are different in quality from those by westerners, so the whole mood of soul of Rabindranath Tagore is different from that of a European or an American. And this is because even an educated modern oriental, if he has been schooled in the Orient, evades this deeper connection with the physical body. Here lies a temptation, one now of a luciferic kind, to fail to make full use of the human physical body. Whereas an American strives to employ the full scope of the physical body, the oriental seeks to employ it too little.

This is how we should understand the psychology of diverse

peoples nowadays. Decades ago, the global catastrophe might have been avoided if people had considered the relationship between the people of western and eastern Europe. Back in 1910 I had very good reason for speaking of the folk spirits.[58] This lecture cycle contains various insights into elements that have contributed to the catastrophic world war of the last five years. In all these things it is really a matter of preparing oneself, very seriously, so that we do not evade reality but comprehend it fully: that we place ourselves into evolution in a way that goes beyond the confines of self-involved egoism in which we consider only our most immediate surroundings. We cannot meet the task facing us today if we do not find the good will to imagine ourselves at least into the whole of humanity's evolution, to be aware of what is unfolding there.

This is not meant to be a critique of the past. I have often said that such a thing must inevitably appear foolish from a spiritual-scientific perspective. What is necessary is the insight that we ought to think and act differently in future than we did in the past, that we must seek to carry forwards into the future what emerges and becomes available to us from spiritual knowledge.

In recent days I have been speaking to you about how we should regard our whole life between birth and death. As we enter life at birth, we bring with us into sensory, physical existence supersensible powers from our supersensible existence. These powers go on working. This is something that people today find very difficult to conceive of. How do they go on working? They do so in everything we develop in this physical world as the life of the mind, of human culture and spirit. If we could not bring with us at birth impulses originating in pre-birth life there would be no possibility of having poets amongst us, or of developing a world-view or science, or a human education. Spiritual, cultural life originates in pre-birth existence. By contrast, what we develop from will impulses within economic life, all that we do in a sense unawares simply by participating in economic life—fraternity, love of humanity, thinking not just for ourselves but for others, working not just for ourselves but for others—supplies us with the most important impulses we bear with us back into the world of spirit. Just as we bear with us from the world of spirit powers which primarily constitute our life of spirit here on earth, so we carry back into the world of spirit the powers we develop in economic life as human love and fraternity. They accompany us and become important impulses for us there. If we study what emerges year by year in a child's life, we can find in it the legacy of what originates in the world of spirit so that a person can unfold here his spiritual inclinations. And if we study what occurs in economic life, in the form of work performed for others through our will, at the same time we discover in it what we bear back with us into the world of spirit when we pass once more through the gate of death. And what develops only between our birth and death appears, to someone who can perceive the world of spirit, as the opposite of what develops only in the spiritual world between death and rebirth.

If you read what I say in *Theosophy* about soul and spirit land,[59] you will find there an account in terms that originate entirely in living vision of conditions there. But everything that constitutes the rights state, by contrast, is the opposite of impulses at work in the life between death and rebirth. We establish our life of culture and spirit with powers that originate in the time prior to birth or conception, while we develop economic life so that we can bear the powers thus engendered into the world of spirit again; and what is developed only here and belongs to the earth alone is the political dimension, the legislative life of the state, and this has no connection with the world of spirit at all.

People generally make things easy for themselves by interpreting the things involved in these domains in the way they are capable of doing. Many people today apply to present conditions the biblical phrase 'Render unto Caesar what is Caesar's and unto God what is God's', possibly in order to hearken back a little to monarchical values in these republican times. Yet this is a phrase that cannot easily be applied to our modern times but can only properly be understood in its intrinsic context. The Roman Caesar was himself a god in those days, and required worship owed to the divine. Caligula[60] even demanded this divine worship by having the Greek statues brought to Rome—only the statue of Zeus was saved—and ordering that their heads be struck off and replaced with the head of Caligula. He thought this was a fitting thing to do. When Jesus of Nazareth spoke this phrase, he intended it to mean this: Give to Caesar what belongs to Caesar yet hold back something for the god you must seek in a being other than Caesar's. Many Gospel passages have to be transposed rightly into our own times and interpreted somewhat differently from usual. Then we can increasingly wrestle our way through to a grasp of reality that we need today.

Over these days I undertook to highlight various aspects of our human task in the modern era: to wrestle our way through to this perception of reality which we can only attain by regarding spiritual reality as something of equal validity alongside sensory reality. The greatest harm nowadays is caused by shutting our eyes to reality. For a long time now people have not run politics in a 'politic' way, but shut their eyes to what is real. Anthroposophically oriented spiritual science seeks something of vital importance: an opening of our eyes to reality. As one can witness nowadays, these eyes have mostly still hardly opened at all. People say the most extraordinary things which testify to their lack of any sense of reality. Please do not misunderstand me—I have to draw your attention to these things because they illustrate our times. Various individuals closely connected with the events that have brought such misfortune over central Europe—which has not ended in fact, but is only in its infancy—only revealed their true colours during the terrible events of the summer of 1918, especially also the autumn of that year. Various people who are responsible for much of this misfortune finally showed their true countenance at this point. These people found themselves in strange situations—strange because their situations had changed. I have met people who now contemplate with some regret the current situation in which these responsible individuals find themselves, but do not think of asking whether there are not, after all, countless millions of people in the world today who are suffering far more, both bodily and psychologically, than merely altered circumstances. In relation to such things it is important to open our eyes and give serious attention to the need to perceive truly. Pie-in-the-sky-ism means pursuing certain preferred ideas that are easy and comfortable to entertain without actually taking any account of what reality is telling us. It is not easy or comfortable to speak the truth about such things today. But having had to witness, with a bleeding heart, how things have taken their course, how pie-in-the-sky-ism had such devastating effects whereas what looked reality squarely in the face was regarded as mere utopian idealism,[61] I am obliged to focus on these things. Now that things stand fully revealed in the light of day in our tormented central Europe, our sympathy and compassion should not prevent us from pointing to fantasists such as Ludendorff[62] who never wanted to see reality as it is but sought to make it conform to his own ideas of how it should be. In this realm too we must be clear-eyed in our perceptions of reality, of the great scope of these matters, which are not of small importance. All these attempts, in bad taste, to justify oneself before the world amount to the bitterest accusations and complaints. No healing will come until people realize the importance of these things and the vital need to see their reality. I did not come here in order to hint at them in a subtle, tactful way. A spiritual-scientific movement is of serious import, and I feel obliged to speak plainly. Our mouths have been locked as Papageno's was, and we had to stand by silently as Michaelis[63] played out his arts of governance over the last four or five years, appointing people of utter inability to ruling posts. These things are all part of the picture, and stand there like shadows alongside the great truths which inevitably stream through all humanity.

I know that many people feel wounded when one urges them to face the truth about such things. But we cannot go on putting our heads in the sand. Only by looking squarely at the truth will we find the strength that can help humanity progress. We need this strength. We need to comprehend something fundamentally at odds with the views of those who have brought humanity to such a pass. We have to have the courage to grasp things anew, and what I have said here and elsewhere in anthroposophic gatherings is a preparation for doing so. I had no wish to offer a better kind of Sunday sermon, if you like, but to convey to you the earnest needs of our time. To be an anthroposophist in the real meaning of the word means to be at the very pulse of contemporary developments, to seek the truth and not to make do with lies which have so gravely entangled us at present. I trust I have been able to reach your hearts with the few words with which I sought to characterize the opposite, the shadow aspect, of what is needed. I was not speaking to your rational minds alone, but above all to your hearts, for the broad understanding of our age that we need must come from the heart. We must find the impulses that can set humanity upon its feet again, but to do this we must first recognize the depth to which empty phrases have entangled us in all realms of life. Truth will come from the spirit. Wisdom can be found in truth alone.[64] This is something we should inscribe deeply into our souls.

I have said things to describe modern human nature, specifically characterizing our era of humanity's evolution from a spiritual perspective. I have presented them because I believe that what is most necessary today can be brought home to human hearts through such things: a mood of soul which can give rise to the seriousness necessary if we are to live in service to humanity. During my stay here I set myself the task of invoking in you a sense, a feeling, of this seriousness.

LECTURE 9

IN speaking to a larger audience of the most important questions of our time, much will depend on whether or not we know something of the deeper powers at work in world-historical developments, or in other words of the science of initiation as we may call it. Nowadays it is relatively easy to discuss contemporary issues based on all kinds of outward knowledge that one may consider to be scientific and practically useful. But it is extremely difficult to speak of these questions today once one knows something about this science of initiation, and bases upon it, as one must, everything that we discuss on such occasions as this. Someone who addresses contemporary issues from the point of view of initiation science will be aware that he is opposed not only by the subjective opinions of most of those to whom he is speaking but that a large portion of humanity today is in one way or another also subject to the very powerful, and ever-growing, influence of ahrimanic forces at work in the world. However, I can only explain what I mean by this by offering you first a kind of historical overview of a large span of human history.

From diverse reflections we have engaged in together here, and from various published lecture cycles, you will know that the middle of the fifteenth century marks the beginning of our current era as modern human beings. We have always referred to this period starting around the mid-fifteenth century—which is still basically in its infancy—as the fifth post-Atlantean epoch. It succeeded the previous era which we reckon from the middle of the eighth century BC up to the middle of the fifteenth century. Looking still further back we come to the Egyptian-Chaldean epoch. I mention this in passing only to remind you of the larger context of our modern developments, as we experience them. Now as you know, the Mystery of Golgotha occurred after the first third of the Graeco-Roman epoch. We have described from many different perspectives what occurred through this Mystery of Golgotha and what significance it had for all human evolution, and in fact for the whole evolution of the earth. Today I want to connect certain things relating to this Mystery of Golgotha to this broader historical context.

To do so, let us look back to much more ancient times—let us say to around the beginning of the third millennium BC. As you know, outward historical records have very little to say about this early evolution of the human race on earth. External documents point us to the Orient, to Asia. And from various anthroposophic reflections you will know that the further back we look in humanity's evolution the more different we find the human psyche, and that in a sense we find an ancient primordial wisdom underlying all human evolution at that time. You know that traditional wisdom was preserved within small, secret circles until the nineteenth century, and then, albeit with little correspondence to the primordial wisdom of ancient traditions, until our own day. People today who become acquainted with one or another aspect of this ancient, primordial wisdom of humanity are astonished at the depths of reality to which it points. At the same time, you will have seen from our reflections over the years that these widespread teachings of ancient times contrast radically with the outlooks of the ancient Hebrew peoples, the Jewish people, which are quite different in character. In a sense therefore it is valid to say that the former, widespread, primordial teachings are a heathen element contrasting with Hebrew and Jewish teachings. As you know from extant historical records and documents, the Christian element subsequently emerged from this Jewish tradition.

From these historical facts you can see something that I wish to consider today: that in the course of human evolution it became necessary to oppose an ancient, heathen element and its primordial wisdom with the Jewish element from which Christianity at least partly later developed. In other words, this ancient heathen wisdom was not granted sole influence over humanity's further evolution. And this will lead us to ask why it was that this ancient, primordial, heathen wisdom, which in many respects can elicit our wonder, had to acquire a new shape, had to be transformed through Judaism and Christianity.

This is a question we need to ask, but for initiation wisdom it can be answered only by a very, very important fact, an occurrence in the Far East at the beginning of the third millennium BC. Looking back to these times in inward vision, the seer discovers there too the human incarnation of a supersensible being—like the incarnation of a supersensible being occurring through the Mystery of Golgotha, when Christ entered the human being Jesus of Nazareth. The incarnation that occurred at the beginning of the third millennium BC is extremely hard to perceive even with the spiritual-scientific vision made possible by initiation science. It endowed humankind with something extraordinarily luminous, extraordinarily incisive— basically that ancient, primordial wisdom which I referred to.

From an initially outward perspective, one can say that this influx of wisdom, deeply penetrating reality, was cold, intellectual, little coloured by a content of feeling or sensibility. But that is an external appraisal. We can only inwardly judge the nature of this wisdom if we look back to the incarnation that occurred in the Far East, in Asia, at the start of the third millennium BC. Here we discover by clair- voyant vision that the power of Lucifer did truly incarnate into humanity; and that this incarnation, accomplished in a certain way, gave rise to a primordial wisdom that spread amongst human culture in the third post-Atlantean epoch.

What this Asiatic and luciferic cultural impulse spread amongst humanity worked on into the ancient Greek era: a luciferic wisdom that was certainly of benefit to humankind at that phase of evolution, and was in some ways illustrious. It manifests in a range of nuances depending on the different peoples and races amongst whom it spread, clearly discernible throughout Asia and still apparent in Egyptian and Babylonian culture, but, as I said, also underlying the foundations of Greek culture. Everything that human beings could think, compose and will at the time was in a sense determined by this luciferic impetus in human culture.

It would of course be extremely narrow-minded to say that since this was an incarnation of Lucifer we should want nothing to do with it. Such philistinism would lead us to flee all kinds of things of great beauty and grandeur that emerged in humanity from this Lucifer stream. As stated, the ideal of Greek beauty also arose from this developmental stream. At the time the Mystery of Golgotha unfolded, all Gnostic thinking and knowledge then existing was a penetrating wisdom that profoundly illumined the world and drew on the impulse of luciferic powers. We cannot therefore say that this Gnostic thinking was misguided. To say it was imbued with luciferic impulses is merely to characterize it.

Now, two millennia and a good deal more after this incarnation of Lucifer came the Mystery of Golgotha. And we can say that the thinking, feeling and sensibilities of those amongst whom the impulse of the Mystery of Golgotha spread were still fully endowed with the quality of this luciferic impulse. But now a very different quality of impulse arose, that of Christ, and entered the evolutionary stream of civilization. We have often spoken of its significance within humanity. Today I will just say in passing that the Christ impulse was absorbed by sensibilities of the kind I described. We can put it like this: the Christ impulse shone its light into the best of Lucifer's endowments to humanity. In the early Christian centuries the Christ impulse was absorbed, the Christ was understood, by virtue of what humankind had received from Lucifer. We have to be open-minded about these things, otherwise we will never properly understand the distinctive way in which the Christ impulse was absorbed in these early centuries.

As the luciferic impulse increasingly faded from human sensibility, people grew ever less capable of fully absorbing the true nature of the

Christ impulse. You need only consider the increasing materialism that prevailed as the modern era advanced. But if you ask what became most materialistic of all, you have to acknowledge that it was modern Christian theology. You see, a great part of modern Christian theology testifies to the greatest materialism: it no longer sees the Christ living in the human being Jesus of Nazareth but refers to him as 'the simple man of Nazareth', a figure more easily understood. The more people accepted the human being Jesus of Nazareth as an ordinary mortal, albeit one amongst the ranks of other renowned historical individuals, the more this pleased a certain materialistic school of modern theology, which wishes to have very little indeed to do with the supersensible nature of the Golgotha event.

The luciferic influx into human sensibility gradually faded in the human soul, making way increasingly for what we call the ahrimanic impulse, which will grow ever stronger in the near and also the further future. The ahrimanic impulse derives from beings other than Christ or Lucifer. Yet it is also a supersensible influx, and we could say a supersensible being—there is little distinction—whose influence will become especially powerful, ever more and more so, in the fifth post-Atlantean epoch. If we consider the turbulence of recent years, we will find that it has been caused in particular by ahrimanic powers.

Like the incarnation of Lucifer at the beginning of the third millennium BC, and the Christ incarnation at the time of the Mystery of Golgotha, there will be an incarnation in the West of the being of Ahriman in the third millennium AD, some time after our current life on earth has ended. We only properly comprehend the course of history and human evolution over almost six millennia if we see it in these terms: a luciferic incarnation at one pole, the Christ incarnation in the middle of this period, and the incarnation of Ahriman at the other pole. Lucifer is the power in us which stirs up all quixotic and fervent powers, all false mysticism, all that seeks to elevate us arrogantly beyond our actual capacities. In a sense it brings our blood into chaotic disorder in order to lift us out of ourselves. Ahriman on the other hand is the power that makes a person prosaic, hardheaded, philistine, that ossifies us and persuades us of the illusory truth of materialism. Basically our human nature is the effort to maintain equilibrium between the luciferic and the ahrimanic power; and in modern times, the Christ impulse aids us in creating this balance or equilibrium. These two poles are always present in us, the luciferic and the ahrimanic. But in historical terms, we find that the luciferic impulse predominated in certain streams of cultural evolution in the pre-Christian period, and through into the early Christian centuries, whereas Ahriman has been active since the mid-fifteenth century, and is growing ever stronger, until eventually an actual incarnation of Ahriman will occur within western humanity.

Now it is intrinsic to such things that they are long prepared beforehand. Just as Lucifer once appeared in human form in China, and Christ Jesus appeared in human form in the Near East, so ahrimanic powers are preparing human evolution in a way that will allow humanity to succumb to Ahriman when he eventually appears in human form in western civilization—which will scarcely any longer be civilization as we know it. There is no use entertaining illusions about such things. Ahriman will appear in human form. All that will matter is the degree to which he finds humankind prepared for his arrival: whether his preparations will enable him to enlist all humanity, all civilization as we know it, to follow his dictates, or whether he will find a humanity that can offer him resistance. Illusions are of no help here. Nowadays people try to evade the truth, and one cannot present it to them plain and unvarnished because they would mock and ridicule such ideas. But nor can one present such things to them as I tried to do now in the form of the threefold social organism.[65] The majority of them at least do not wish to hear about this either. In fact, this refusal to countenance such things is one of the means that ahrimanic powers can employ to ensure that when Ahriman appears in human form he will have the greatest possible number of adherents on earth. This refusal to engage with the most important truths will pave the way for Ahriman to thrive in his incarnation.

You see, in seeking the right stance towards what will unfold in human evolution through Ahriman, nothing will help except an open-minded perception of the powers which Ahriman employs to act upon us, as well as the powers that can arm humanity against the temptations and ensnarements of ahrimanic powers. Today therefore let us cast a look, at least, from various perspectives, on the kinds of things that would consolidate people's adherence to Ahriman, and which now, especially, the ahrimanic powers are sending down from supersensible worlds, sending also through human sensibilities, in order to secure as great a following as possible.

One such means is to obstruct people's understanding of the importance for the human being of certain prevalent types of thinking. You know that there was a huge difference between the way a person felt in relation to the whole cosmos in, say, Egyptian times, and still in Greek times, and how he felt at the beginning of the modern era, after the medieval period had ended. If you imagine an ancient Egyptian fully versed in these things, he would have known that he is not only bodily constituted of substances found here on earth, manifest in the animal, plant and mineral kingdoms, but that his being was informed by an influx of powers that he saw above in the stars. He felt himself to be part of the whole cosmos. He felt the whole cosmos to be not only animate but also ensouled and spiritualized; and in his awareness there lived something of the spiritual entelechies of the cosmos, the soul nature of the cosmos, the life of the cosmos. All this was lost in the course of modern human history. Today the human being gazes up from his earth to the starry world where he sees planets, stars, suns, comets and so forth. But what means does he use to observe everything he sees up there in the cosmos, all that gazes down upon him? He uses mathematics, and at most also mechanical laws. Everything that encompasses the earth is now void of spirit, soul and even life for him.

The cosmos is now seen, really, as a great mechanical construct that can only be understood with the aid of mathematical and mechanical laws. Employing these laws we understand it wonder-fully well! This is not to say that a spiritual scientist will not fully value the achievements of Galileo, Kepler and others. But what enters human comprehension and human awareness through the teachings of these great figures reveals the universe to be nothing but a vast mechanism.

What this means for our view of reality can be seen only by someone able to trace the full scope of human nature. Astronomers and astrophysicists posit the universe as a mechanism that can be comprehended and calculated through mathematical formulae, and a world-view such as this is one people can certainly credit from the moment they wake up in the morning to when they fall asleep again at night. But in the unconscious depths people do not reach with their waking consciousness, but which belong to their existence nevertheless, and in which they live during sleep, a quite different sense of things, a different comprehension of the universe, flows into the human soul. A knowledge then lives within us that we are not consciously aware of but that lives below in the depths of our soul and configures it—a knowledge of the spirit, of the life of the soul, of the life of the cosmos. And while people are unaware in their waking consciousness of what occurs in them in community with the spirit, soul and life of the universe from the time they fall asleep to the moment they wake up, these things nevertheless live in the soul. Much of the split in modern human beings is caused by the dis-harmony between the soul's experience of the universe during sleep and its avowed view of the universe in waking awareness.

The whole spirit and import of anthroposophically oriented spiritual science tells you that while Galileo and Copernicus intro-duced into humanity a view of the universe that is grandiose and mighty this is not an absolute truth but just *one* aspect of the cos-mos—one way of looking at it. It is arrogant of modern humankind to say that the Ptolemaic system is childish, that people thought like this when humanity was still in its infancy. The idea that we have now attained some kind of absolute truth through our 'glorious advancements'[66] is mistaken. This world-view is no more absolute than the Ptolemaic system was: just one perspective. Anthro-posophically oriented spiritual science can teach us that mere 'cosmic mathematics', all schemata of a mechanical kind, do not provide us with an absolute truth but give us illusions about the cosmos. This is not to say that we do not need these illusions—they are intrinsic to the particular evolutionary stage we are passing through, and educative for us, as other views were intrinsic to other stages and educative. We have to appropriate them, but we must also know that they are illusory. And they become even more illusory when we carry them on into our everyday surroundings in atomistic teachings about matter, finding a kind of small-scale astronomy in molecular theory, in the nature of the earth's substances. A true perspective on modern science, wherever it posits such things, will recognize that this is all founded on illusion.

Ahriman, hoping that his incarnation will be as fruitful as possible for him, is most keenly interested in human beings perfecting this illusory science, which more or less accounts for all science today, but without them realizing that it is illusory. Ahriman has the very greatest interest in teaching people mathematics but without them seeing that mathematical and mechanical views of the cosmos are mere illusion. He has the very greatest interest in teaching humanity chemistry, physics, biology and so forth, which figure in our culture as greatly admired disciplines, but to make us believe, too, that they embody absolute truths rather than partial aspects—photographs if you like from only one viewpoint. If you photograph a tree from one side only, it will give you a true yet only a partial image. A fuller picture will emerge if you photograph it from four sides. Ahriman has the profoundest interest in concealing from humanity the fact that modern intellectual and rationalist science, with its credo of empiricism, is a great illusion. He would secure supreme, triumphant success if he could succeed in perpetuating into the third millennium these scientific superstitions so prevalent everywhere today, which even dictate the terms of social science. Born then as a human being, he would rejoice to find these scientific superstitions living within western civilization.

But do not draw the wrong conclusions from what I have now said. It would be mistaken to simply avoid and evade modern science—that would be the most misguided thing you could do. We should fully acquaint ourselves with it, but with full awareness that it offers us an illusory aspect, albeit necessary and educative for us at this stage of our evolution. We do not defend ourselves against Ahriman by avoiding modern science but rather by acquainting ourselves with its true form and nature. This science inevitably gives us an outward illusion about the cosmos, and we need this. Please do not think that we do not need this outward illusion. But from a quite different angle and perspective, through spiritual research, we must fill it with true reality, advancing from its illusory character to the real truth. Numerous lecture cycles I have given emphasize what I am saying again today: I have always tried to engage fully with modern science, yet at the same time to lift it higher into the realm where we can perceive the extent to which it holds true. To wish away modern science is rather like wishing away a rainbow just because it is an illusion of light and colour. To understand it fully you will first have to comprehend its illusory character, and the same is true of all the ideas and concepts of the world which modern science offers. It offers only illusions, and we must see through them. By the very fact of penetrating these illusions we educate ourselves to comprehend the world's reality. Keeping humankind locked in its scientific superstitions is one of the means employed by Ahriman to make his incarnation as effective as possible.

The other means, a second means, is to encourage everything that divides people today, sunders them into small cliques and groupings at odds with one another. In the political arena we can see this clearly today in all the parties and factions. If we study this phenomenon with an open mind we can see that these parties feuding with each other cannot be explained by mere differences in human nature. You can't explain the Great War by referring to human disharmonies between different types of person, or differences of nation and race. Here it is very clear that non-sensory powers—ahrimanic powers— have been exerting their influence.

And these ahrimanic powers are at work wherever disharmonies between groups of people arise. Let us take a very characteristic example to show what most of these things are based upon. Our modern proletariat now looks to Karl Marx.[67] It is worth studying how the teachings of Karl Marx spread amongst the modern pro-letariat, and how they gave rise to a never-ending flood of Marxist literature. This literature fully embraces the scientific mode— everything is rigorously supported with proof and evidence, so rigorously in fact that many one would have thought immune to Marxism have in fact succumbed to it. The fate of Marxism was to spread, first of all, through the proletariat, while academic institu-tions disputed and rejected it. Now there are a number of academics who can no longer resist the logic of Marxism, who acknowledge it and can no longer escape it, because Marxist literature, as has gradually become apparent, offers subtly congruent conclusions. With a modern scientific outlook and mode of thinking, the propositions of Marxism can be very nicely proven. The middle classes did not have their own Karl Marx to prove the opposite. But it would have been possible. You see, just as one can prove the ideo-logical character of law and ethics, etc., and the theory of added value, and axioms of materialistic history from a Marxist perspective, so one could equally well prove exactly the opposite about all such things. It would be perfectly possible for a bourgeois Marx to prove exactly the opposite in the same rigorous way, without any distortion or underhand aims. Such evidence would certainly stand up.

And this is because modern human thinking, the modern intellect, lies in a stratum of our being that prevents it reaching down to access realities. This is why one can prove one thing and then its opposite equally well, both with an equally rigorous procedure. Today it is possible, with equally valid logic, to prove the truth of spiritualism on the one hand and materialism on the other. These conflicting perspectives can feud with each other with equal right because modern intellectualism lives in an upper stratum of reality and does not plumb the depths of existence. The same applies to partisan viewpoints of all kinds. If we do not comprehend this but simply absorb such things through our upbringing, family, through the particular conditions we live in and the politics of the day, we may honestly believe our partisan view to be well founded and yet we have just fallen or slipped into it, and find ourselves in conflict with people who have likewise slipped into their own partisan position. Both positions will be equally valid, and this brings chaos and confusion over humanity. The convulsions it causes will continually increase if humanity does not come to see this. And this confusion is something that ahrimanic powers employ, again, to prepare their triumphant incarnation, driving humankind ever more strongly into something it finds so difficult to comprehend: that one thing and its very opposite can be equally proven with the same, well-founded intellectual or scientific reasoning. We have to recognize that anything can be proven, and it is in this light that we should see the proofs hammered out in modern academic discourse. Only in a science in the strict meaning of the word, the strict study of phenomena, can realities become apparent. But in no other field should one allow merely intellectual proofs to hold sway. Human knowledge and perception must be sought at a deeper level—as in the practice of anthroposophically oriented spiritual science—than in the stratum of our being where evidence and proof originates. And only then can we avoid the danger of succumbing to the ahrimanic temptation that increasingly drags us down into these things. In our era Ahriman also uses everything founded on genetics and inheritance to sow confusion and discord, although we have really grown beyond this now in the fifth post-Atlantean epoch. The ahrimanic power employs all that originates in heredity to set groups of human beings at odds with each other. Everything based on differences of family, race and nation is used by the ahrimanic powers to sow discord. It is a fine thing to preach freedom for every race and nation, even the smallest, but adversarial powers always employ fine words to sow confusion and to achieve the things that Ahriman wishes to for his incarnation.

Who is it who incites nation against nation and invokes the kinds of issues that dominate humanity today? It is Ahriman, the ahrimanic seduction influencing people. People are so easily deceived in this domain. They do not wish to descend to the deeper strata where realities exist. Ahriman is ably preparing for his aims. Since the

Reformation and Renaissance, the prevailing view of the human being in modern culture has been that of 'economic man', and rulers have been those with economic power. You can trace this clearly in history. If you go further back in history to ancient times, even to the era I spoke of as luciferic in character, the rulers were initiates! The Egyptian pharaohs, the Babylonian rulers, the rulers of Asia, were initiates. Then the era of priests emerged, of priest kings, and they were dominant basically until the Reformation and Renaissance. Since then economic man holds sway, and rulers are only the agents of economic factors. We must not think that modern rulers are anything other than the agents of economic man. And all the laws that have been created—it is worth studying this carefully—are simply a consequence of what economists have thought. Not until the nineteenth century do we see banking ideas and bankers replacing economic factors; and only then is the whole social order created which overlays and hides all other social conditions by means, really, of the money economy. It is just a question of seeing these things clearly, and tracing them in an empirical, phenomenological way.

Everything I said in my second public lecture here is profoundly true.[68] We should study all the details of these things—and if we do so will discover them to be thoroughly true. Specifically as the dominance of a mere 'symbol for genuine goods' emerged, a major ahrimanic deception surfaced with it. If we do not understand that we must counter 'economic man' and the economic order established by bankers with the legislative state and the spiritual organism of society, Ahriman will, once again, find in this failure of perception a substantial means to prepare the triumph of his incarnation, which is certainly underway and will arrive. These are the kinds of means Ahriman can use, drawing on a certain type of person. However there is also another type—though often both types are present in one and the same person—who helps to smooth his triumphant progress.

You see, complete errors in real life are not actually as harmful as half and quarter truths. Things completely mistaken soon become apparent while half and quarter truths seduce people: they live with them and these partial truths worm their way into life and have the most devastating effects.

There are people who do not recognize that the world-view of Galileo and Copernicus are partial truths, do not perceive their illusory nature, or find it too arduous to engage with them at all. We have shown already how misguided this is. But there are also people today, a great many of them, who acknowledge a certain half-truth, a very important one, and refuse to recognize that it is only true within certain limits. Just as it is partial and one-sided to acknowledge the world only as Galileo and Copernicus describe it, or more generally in terms of academic disciplines of a materialistic kind, so it is likewise one-sided to acknowledge the world only as it is presented in the Gospels, and to refuse any other approach to truth and reality. The Gospels were of course given to those who lived in the first centuries of Christianity.

To believe, today, that the Gospels can give us the whole of Christianity is a half-truth, and therefore one that continually befuddles people, offering Ahriman the best means to achieve the goal, the triumphant conquest, of his incarnation.

There are a great many people nowadays who believe they are speaking in Christian humility when they say that they have no need of spiritual science. In fact this is terrible arrogance. The simplicity and plain-speaking of the Gospels, they say, leads them to the eternal truths humankind needs. It is usually actually real arrogance that comes to expression in such seeming humility, and this proves very useful to Ahriman in the way I have suggested. Please do not forget what I said at the start of today's reflections—that at the time when the Gospels were written, people's thinking, feeling and vision, their whole way of seeing things, was imbued with a luciferic quality. They were able to grasp the Gospels in terms of a kind of luciferic gnosis; but nowadays we can no longer grasp the Gospels in this ancient way. To hammer on about the Gospels as they have been handed down to us will no longer give us a real comprehension of Christ. A true view of Christ is in fact nowhere less forthcoming than in the diverse religious confessions. For us to come to a real understanding of Christ today the Gospels need to be deepened through spiritual science. Here it is interesting to study the separate Gospels carefully and fathom their true content. But just to take the Gospels at face value, as many people are nowadays taught to do, is not a path towards Christ but a path away from him. This is why the confessions are drifting ever further away from Christ. What view of Christ is found by someone who takes the Gospels at face value without deepening them through spiritual science? If he does really study the Gospels he will ultimately arrive at a form of Christ, but one that falls far short of the reality to which only spiritual science can lead us. The Gospels as they are lead to a correct view of Christ, in a sense, yet this is only a kind of hallucination, a picture or vision if you like, albeit a real inner one, but no more than a picture. We do not find Christ's reality by this means. And this is precisely the reason why modern theology has become so materialistic. Those who study the Gospels merely as theology arrive at the view that what can be gained from them is more or less the same as the conclusion they draw from Paul's Damascene experience. Wishing to establish Christianity, yet in fact undermining it, they state that Paul was sick, mentally ill, and this was why he had his vision at Damascus.

The Gospels alone only enable us to form an hallucination, a vision. Through them we can gain an inwardly true picture but not the reality of Christ. To reach the real Christ we have to fathom everything that we can today gain from spirit knowledge of the world. This is why those who reject any kind of true spiritual knowledge and perception, and in their sectarian confessions hammer on the truth of the Gospels alone, are already forming the beginnings of a flock for Ahriman when he appears in human form within modern civilization. They reject all spiritual exertions that lead to detailed and tangible perception, and their circles will therefore produce hosts of adherents to Ahriman's cause.

These things are developing and are at work amongst modern humanity. Someone who speaks to humankind today—whether of social questions or other matters—with knowledge of initiation science is speaking in this context and addressing this situation. He knows where the adversarial powers are at work, that they dwell above all in the supersensible realm, and that human beings, poor souls, are succumbing to them, are being led astray. His appeal to humanity will therefore be this: let us try to free ourselves from the grave temptations that seek to enlist us in establishing and consolidating the triumph of Ahriman.

There are many who feel something along these lines, but there is not yet enough courage to fully engage, as anthroposophic spiritual science must, with Christ, and the historical impulses of Lucifer and Ahriman in the thorough way that is needed. People sense the need for this but they hold back from going far enough. Where today can we find recognition of the need to penetrate worldly, materialistic science and its ahrimanic character with the Christ impulse, and on the other hand to illumine the Gospels through spiritual-scientific insights? How many people are really working to do both the one and other through true spiritual-scientific endeavours? Yet humanity will only gain the right stance towards Ahriman's earthly incarnation by comprehending these things, at the same time finding the courage, will and energy to shine the spirit into worldly science and to illumine the Gospels with this same spirit. Otherwise only half-truths will emerge. Think for instance of an enlightened figure such as Cardinal Newman,[69] who had clear vision of modern religious developments. When he was invested as Cardinal in Rome, he openly stated in his address that to survive into the future Christian, Catholic teachings would need a new revelation. But we do not need a new revelation, for the age of revelations in the old sense has passed. Instead, we need a new science that is illumined by the spirit.

But people need the courage to engage with this new science.

Think for instance of a literary series such as *Lux Mundi* around the end of the 1880s, the beginning of the 1890s.[70] Certain members of the English High Church, renowned theologians that belonged to it, sought to build bridges between worldly disciplines and religious dogma. But this amounted only to a tentative, tenuous effort rather than a keen grasp of worldly science, a real illumining of it by the spirit, an open-minded study of the Gospels. Nowhere was it clearly stated that the Gospels alone are no longer enough, that they need illumining and clarifying. But that is what modern humanity needs: a two-pronged courage that says worldly science alone leads to illusion, and the Gospels alone lead to hallucination. We will only find a middle way between illusion and hallucination in a real, spiritually informed grasp of reality. That is what counts.

It is important to penetrate these things with understanding. A merely worldly science would sow nothing but illusion amongst humanity and would lead people eventually to accomplish nothing but idiocies. There is already enough stupidity in the world—the Great War was, surely, a great stupidity. Many of those involved in it were imbued with the outlooks of modern science. And if you look at the curious symptoms that appear when, for instance, some sect or other places unique emphasis on one of the four Gospels alone, you will more easily understand what I have said today about the Gospels. A sect that hearkens only to the Gospel of St John, or another that does the same with the Gospel of St Luke, tends strongly, as you can discover, to all kinds of hallucinatory symptoms. The one-sided nature of each Gospel, thank goodness, has not yet sown calamity, because there are four Gospels which outwardly contradict each other. Because there are four Gospels people cannot succumb to the direction of one alone, cannot be drawn exclusively in that direction. One Sunday a priest will read from one of them, the next from another, and this mitigates the effect of each, complementing and modifying it with that of the others. There is great wisdom in the fact that these four Gospels have come down to us, so that—unlike many adherents of sects—we do not succumb to a single current that would overwhelm us if we studied only one Gospel alone. If we allow only one of the Gospels to work upon us it becomes especially evident that this will ultimately lead to hallucinatory symptoms.

Yes, we have to shed a good deal of our subjective inclinations, a good deal of what we feel naturally drawn to, which we consider to be pious or clever. Of primary importance today is for us to develop an all-round sense of the truth; and for this, courage is required.

That is what I wished to say to you today so that you can realize that what we are trying to achieve within humanity does have much deeper roots than merely subjective inclinations or prejudice. It is read from the signs of the times, as something that must be undertaken. It has been a relatively long time since we met together here, and I was very concerned today to say what I now have. I hope that we will have a further opportunity to speak about such things again in the not too distant future.

LECTURE 10

HUMANITY'S current stage of evolution bears a particular character—and of course we can say that every age marks the beginning of an evolutionary phase, but then we must characterize its nature. The character of this new phase into which we are now entering is one which, into the far future of the earth, will inevitably bring humanity an experience of decline and descent in the physical world, a reversal, a retrograde development. We have already passed the time when humanity advanced by virtue of ever more refined physical powers. In forthcoming times humanity will still advance but only through a spiritual evolution that raises itself above the processes of the physical plane. Physical processes will no longer bring satisfaction to those who wish only to give themselves up to them. In the context of our spiritual science we have long since indicated, as described in the lecture cycle on the Apocalypse,[71] that humanity is heading towards a 'war of all against all', and from now onwards this is something that should be taken very, very seriously. It should not remain a merely theoretical truth for people but must come to expression in their actions and whole conduct. The very fact that—to put it trivially—people will gain little pleasure from their evolution on the physical plane in future will increasingly lead them to see that further evolution must instead emerge from spiritual powers.

We will only be able to gain full understanding of these things if we consider a broad span of humanity's evolution, and apply the lessons we learn from this to what humankind will increasingly encounter in future. Then we can see what aims are at work in humanity, coming to expression in rhythmically recurring war and devastation of which the present catastrophe is only a beginning. It would be very short-sighted to think that this catastrophic war[72] will lead in some way to lasting peace enjoyed by humanity on the physical plane. This will not be so. What has to come on earth is spiritual development. And we can see its spirit, its direction and meaning if we survey a relatively long span of time preceding the Mystery of Golgotha, then consider something of the meaning of the Mystery of Golgotha itself, and subsequently try to spiritually trace the further effects of the Mystery of Golgotha in humanity's future evolution.

We have considered the Mystery of Golgotha from the most varied angles, and today I would like to add another perspective by describing something of the character of human civilization preceding the Mystery of Golgotha, going back say to the third millennium before Christ and tracing a quality that lasted into the Christian era and which, as you know, is referred to as heathen culture. Within this heathen culture, like an oasis, arose a very different, Hebraic culture, that of the Jewish people; and from this in turn Christianity emerged.

We can understand heathen culture if we are clear that it was one, basically, whose knowledge, vision and actions drew on more comprehensive powers than earthly ones. We can say that the Hebrew-Judaic culture is what really first inoculated humankind with the moral element, which had no distinct existence in heathen culture. Instead, though, this ancient heathen culture was such that the human being felt himself to be embedded in the whole cosmos. This is something of which we should take particular note. The human being as a participant in ancient heathen culture on earth felt himself to be part of the whole cosmos. He felt how the powers at work in the course of the stars continued on into his own actions or, more accurately, continued in the powers at work in his own actions. The study of astrology, as it later developed and as it survived into our own times, is only a pale reflection and really a very misleading one of this ancient wisdom that was drawn down from the course of the stars and which at the same time dictated human actions. We only properly understand these ancient cultures if, from the perspective of spiritual science, we shed a little light on the outward course of human evolution in the fourth and fifth centuries BC. In speaking of the second and first post-Atlantean eras, and picturing human life on earth then, during the fifth, sixth and seventh millennia BC, we must avoid thinking of it in terms that too closely resemble our own existence today. In these ancient times, people on earth possessed a kind of instinctive soul life that in some respects was closer to the soul life of animals than to our inner experience today. But it would be a very narrow way of seeing things to say merely that people were more animal-like in those times. The human beings on earth in those early times were certainly more animal-like in their state of soul, but these animal bodies of humankind were used by spirit-soul beings, and therefore felt themselves to be very much part of supersensible and above all cosmic worlds. If we look back far enough, to around the fifth millennium BC, human beings did not feel themselves so much to be inhabiting their animal bodies but experienced the latter more as instruments. If we wish to characterize these humans more precisely we must say that when they were awake they did wander around with an instinctive soul life like animals, but into this instinctive soul life shone something like dreams from their sleeping state: something like waking dreams. In these waking dreams they saw how they had descended into their animal bodies but only to use them. The real nature of inner soul experience at that time passed down as vision and rite to Mithraic rituals and worship, whose chief symbol is the god Mithras riding upon a bull: above the starry heavens to which *he* belongs, and below the earthly realm to which the bull belongs. This was not really a symbol for these ancient people but a vision of their reality. A person had this inner experience: outside of my body during the night, I belong to the powers of the cosmos and the starry heavens; on awakening in the morning, I employ the animal instincts in an animal body.

Then a kind of twilight shrouded humanity's evolution. The life of humankind became somewhat duller and more obtuse as the cosmic dreams receded and instinctual life gained the upper hand. The earlier soul state of human beings was preserved within the mysteries, principally those of Asia. But humanity in general, in so far as it did not participate in mystery wisdom, lived in a more or less dull, twilight condition during the fourth and beginning of the third millennium. We can say that at this period, the fourth and beginning of the third millennium BC, a diffuse and twilight soul life existed across Asia and the known world of the time, an instinctive life of soul. But the mysteries existed, and their rites and ceremonies actively enabled the worlds of spirit to flow into human life, thus continuing to illumine human beings by these means.

But now, at the beginning of the third millennium BC, something very significant occurred. In characterizing this twilight and more instinctual life of humankind at the time we can say that the human being's soul-spiritual entelechy was not yet able to make use of intrinsically human organs of understanding and thinking. These organs were already there, had been developed in the human being's physical organism, but his soul-spiritual being could not yet employ them. Thus people could not as yet gain knowledge through their thinking or powers of judgement. Instead they could only gain what was given them through the mysteries.

But now, around the beginning of the third millennium BC, a significant event occurred in the East. Without resistance, a child grew up in one of the wealthy families connected with the rites and ceremonies of the Asiatic mysteries of the time. Circumstances were such that this child was permitted to participate in these ceremonies, no doubt because the priests in charge of the mysteries felt something inspiring them to allow this to such a child. When the person living in this child had grown to be about 40, something remarkable occurred—and it has to be said that the mystery priests in a sense had a prophetic vision that this would happen. Around the age of 40, this person who had grown up within the mysteries of eastern Asia suddenly began to grasp by means of human powers of judgement the meaning of what had formerly only entered the mysteries through revelation. He was more or less the first who might employ the organs of human understanding in this way, and only in relation to the mysteries.

If we translate into our modern language what the priests of the mysteries said about this, we would put it like this: no less a being than Lucifer himself was incarnated in this human being. It is highly significant that in the third millennium BC, in eastern Asia, Lucifer actually incarnated in the flesh in a real sense. This individual, Lucifer incarnate in the flesh, who also then taught others, was the origin of what we now regard as pre-Christian heathen culture, and lived too in the Gnosis of the early Christian centuries. It would be quite wrong to speak in a derogatory way of this Lucifer culture. The beauty that emerged from Greek culture, its philosophical insights, everything at work in ancient Greek philosophy and the tragedies of Aeschylus would not have been possible without this incarnation of Lucifer. As I said, the power and influence of this incarnation worked on also in southern Europe, North Africa and western Asia in the early Christian centuries. And after the Mystery of Golgotha had occurred on earth, it was understood largely through this luciferic wisdom. The Gnosis by means of which the Mystery of Golgotha could initially be grasped was certainly informed and made fruitful by luciferic wisdom. This is what we must stress to begin with: that at the beginning of the third millennium BC Lucifer incarnated in China; then, at the beginning of our era, Christ incarnated, and initially this incarnation of Christ was understood by virtue of the still-present power of that ancient Lucifer incarnation. This power faded from human insight, as a human capacity, during the fourth century AD, and yet it continued to have its after-effects, its reverberations.

And now, in a not-too-distant future, these two incarnations—that of Lucifer in ancient times, and the incarnation of Christ which gives earth evolution its intrinsic meaning—will be joined by a third.

Current events are in large measure preparing this third incarnation. The incarnation of Lucifer in the third millennium BC endowed humankind with the capacity to employ the organs of his thinking, reason and judgement. It was Lucifer himself in a human body who first grasped through rational judgement what formerly could only enter humankind through revelation: the meaning of the mysteries. And what is now being prepared and will quite certainly occur on earth in the not-too-distant future is an actual incarnation of Ahriman.

Since the middle of the fifteenth century, as you know, we have been living in an age when human beings should increasingly come into possession of their full power of awareness. This must be a very significant fact as we approach Ahriman's incarnation: that we do so with full awareness. The incarnation of Lucifer was prophetically perceived only by the mystery priests. And the Christ incarnation through the event at Golgotha was something that remained very largely unconscious to human beings. Now, though, humanity must look consciously towards the approaching incarnation of Ahriman, which will bring with it many traumas on the physical plane. In the ongoing wars and disasters of the near future, the human spirit will become very inventive in the domain of physical life. This will inevitably happen and there is nothing that can be done to avoid it; and this inventiveness will make it possible for Ahriman to incarnate within a bodily human individual.

This ahrimanic potency is preparing its incarnation on earth from the world of spirit. It seeks to prepare this coming incarnation—thus of Ahriman in human form—in a way that will as far as possible enable him to tempt and seduce human beings on earth. As civilization develops in the forthcoming period, our task will be to live with full awareness of the approaching Ahriman incarnation. Then this incarnation of Ahriman can serve humanity through our cultivation of a higher, spiritual evolution, so that we become aware, specifically through Ahriman, of what we can attain, or rather not attain, through merely physical existence. We must live consciously towards this approaching Ahriman incarnation, becoming more conscious in all areas of life, increasingly perceiving what currents in life are drawn towards this incarnation. Through spiritual science people must learn to interpret life so that they perceive and learn to master the currents drawn into the vortex of Ahriman's incarnation. They must know that Ahriman will live amidst humanity on earth but that people can meet him with courage and themselves determine what they can learn from him, what they wish to absorb and accept from him. Yet they will not be able to do this if they do not start now to take the reins of certain spiritual, or unspiritual, currents which Ahriman will otherwise employ to leave human beings as unaware as possible of his arrival. Then he would appear on earth and in a sense overwhelm, tempt and seduce human beings so that they deny earthly evolution and prevent it from reaching its goal. We have to acquaint ourselves with certain spiritual and unspiritual currents if we wish to understand the whole process I have spoken of here.

It is apparent, isn't it, that today increasing numbers of people wish to know nothing about a science of the spirit, about spiritual perception? The old powers of religion, it is clear, no longer act as inner impulse for a great many people. Whether they still attend church or not is no longer of any account to many, for the old powers once active in religion are now devoid of inner meaning for them. But neither do they resolve to encompass the new spiritual life that can flow into our culture. They resist this, reject it, regard it as foolishness, as something they find uncomfortable. They do not engage with it. But actually of course the human being living on earth is a unity and we cannot sunder our spirit from our physical body. Between birth and death they act as one. And if we do not inwardly take up spirit, the spirit is still there nevertheless. Since the last third of the nineteenth century the spiritual element flows everywhere around us, streams into earthly evolution. And one can say that the spirit is there, but that people just do not wish to absorb it.

Even if they do not wish to accept the spirit, it is there nevertheless! It is there. And what happens to this spirit? As paradoxical as it may sound—for much that is true, very true, appears paradoxical to people today—the spirit unconsciously flows into the people who reject or dismiss it. People eat and drink, perhaps those who reject the spirit eat and drink with the greatest gusto, and the spirit flows into the processes of eating and digestion. That is the secret of the path into materialism that began to gather strength around 1840, or rather started to be prepared then. Those who do not absorb spirit through their soul do still absorb it through eating and drinking. They eat and drink the spirit. They are soul and spirit eaters. And in this way the spirit flowing into earth evolution passes into the luciferic element, is conveyed, communicated to Lucifer. By this means the luciferic power grows ever stronger, and can then help the ahrimanic power in preparing its incarnation. Human beings must become aware of this—those at least who are willing to acknowledge that in future people will either absorb spirit knowledge or instead unconsciously consume the spirit and thereby pass it to the luciferic powers. This stream of spirit and soul consumption is especially supportive to Ahriman because he can increasingly lull people asleep in consequence. When he incarnates he will then appear amongst human beings in a way that overwhelms them and prevents them consciously encountering him.

But besides this, Ahriman can directly prepare his incarnation, and is doing so. People today have a life of the spirit, a life of the mind, but a purely intellectual one that does not refer or relate to the world of spirit. This merely intellectual life is spreading amongst humankind increasingly. It first took root in academic life and science, but is now also leading to all kinds of social aberrations in society. What is the nature of this intellectual life? It has so little to do with the real interests of human beings. Let me ask you this: how many professors or teachers are there today in centres of learning, schools and universities who show no real inner enthusiasm for their subject but pursue it simply as a career? The soul's immediate interest does not connect with the study or work undertaken in these places. This even affects children's learning. Just think how much people learn and absorb at various stages of life without having any real interest or enthusiasm in this learning, how superficial and external intellectual life becomes for many who dedicate themselves to it. Think how many people are hard at work producing all sorts of intellectual content that is then preserved in archives and libraries but has no spiritual life. All this intellectual life of the mind, infused with no glowing warmth of soul, devoid of human enthusiasm, directly supports the incarnation of Ahriman and its intrinsic meaning. This lulls people asleep in the way I have described, and can greatly benefit Ahriman.

Alongside this there are many other currents in spiritual, or unspiritual, life that Ahriman can employ if human beings do not themselves use them in the right way. In recent times it has been trumpeted abroad—and is still being proclaimed—that nation states should be established, national realms. One hears a great deal about the 'self-determination of nations'. And yet the time when kingdoms were founded based on blood and race is over now, has no more part to play in our evolution. When people appeal to distinctions of race and nation, which do not arise from the intellect or spirit, this cultivates disharmony amongst humankind. Such disharmony is something the ahrimanic power can very especially use. National chauvinism, distorted patriotism, will provide the material for Ahriman to forge the conditions he seeks.

As well as this, all kinds of party political views are aired today. These partisan views and opinions produce a kind of smokescreen that obscures the gaze for many who do not even wish to see things clearly. Nowadays it is possible to prove anything, even the most radical statements, with great ingenuity. One can prove the truth of Leninism with ingenious arguments, but the opposite can equally well be proven, as well as everything that lies between two such extreme positions. The value of any partisan political programme, and its very reverse, can be proven most rigorously. Both will be right in terms of their arguments. The intellectual spirit that holds sway today is nowhere near adequate for demonstrating whether something has inner vitality, an inner value for life. It proves things, backs them up with evidence; but what is thus proven may still be very far removed from having any intrinsic value or vitality.

Nowadays, therefore, people hold fast to their contrary opinions, their conflicting partisan views, since every such view can be asserted intellectually with equal validity. The nature of the modern intellect is to remain superficial in its grasp of things, rather than penetrating below the surface to where reality prevails. People need only recognize this, fully and thoroughly. They love staying on the surface with their rational outlook rather than penetrating more deeply into other strata of existence in a way that actually corresponds to reality. To confirm this one need only look around a little—even the most superficial glance can show that what human beings love today so easily deceives them. They love numerical values in science, and also in their study of social conditions. Take a look at socialist literature; it is almost entirely composed of statistics, or in other words numbers, and these are used to resolve and investigate the most important aspects of life. Using numbers, anything and everything can be proven, and people can be persuaded of anything. Actually, numbers used in this way are not a means to prove anything but a way of deceiving people. One can be most deceived the moment one no longer looks through and beyond numbers to perceive qualities and realities.

Here is one apt example. There has been much dispute about the nationality of the Macedonian people. A great deal in the politics of the Balkan peninsula relied on the statistical evidence compiled about it. The numbers involved here are as relevant as the numbers used in other statistics. Whether one is studying wheat and rye statistics or the number of people of Greek, Serbian and Bulgarian nationality who live in Macedonia, what statistics can prove is all much of a muchness. Numbers are quoted for the Greek, Serbian and Bulgarian population, and fine conclusions can be drawn from these figures. Or alternatively one can look beyond them and see what is really going on; and this will reveal, for instance, that in any Macedonian family the father may be said to be Greek, while one son is recorded as a Bulgarian and another as a Serbian. How this happens is something you can try to imagine. Such statistics are compiled and quoted in different ways to support different partisan views—and that is all that these statistics are good for. It is obvious that if a father is Greek then both his sons will be too. This is just an example of how the figures are massaged and how numbers are distorted to serve particular ends. Numbers are an element that most help Ahriman to achieve his ends when they are cited as proof and evidence.

A further means that Ahriman can employ is one which is not likely to be immediately recognized as such. It will sound paradoxical. As you know we have tried to study the Gospels more deeply in our spiritual-scientific movement. But this deepening of our understanding of the Gospels, something really increasingly necessary in our time, is dismissed by a great many people just as they reject spiritual science. People who often think—or at least state—that they are humble are in fact the most arrogant. Increasingly it is said one should take the simple message of the Gospels at face value, rather than, say, studying the Mystery of Golgotha in the complex ways that spiritual science proposes. Those who say that they are humble in their search for truth in the Gospels are actually the most arrogant, since they disdain honest and authentic enquiry through spiritual-scientific insights. They are so proud that, without actually exerting themselves, and simply through naive engagement with the Gospels, they believe they can reap the highest knowledge of the world of spirit. What nowadays appears to be simple and humble often clothes the greatest arrogance. The proudest and most arrogant people can be found in sectarian religious confessions.

You see, the Gospels arose at a time when luciferic wisdom still existed. In the early Christian centuries people understood the Gospels in a quite different way from later on. Today those who cannot draw on spiritual science to deepen their understanding merely feign understanding of the Gospels. In reality they do not even know the original meaning of the words written there. The translations into various different languages do not give us the truth of the Gospels. These translations are basically no longer even faintly reminiscent of the original meaning of the words in which the Gospels were first written. Only through spiritual science can we gain real insight into the intervention of the Christ being in earthly evolution. Those who take the 'simple message of the Gospels' at face value, as it is often stated, do not succeed in inwardly comprehending the Christ being but arrive only at an illusion or, at the very most, a vision or hallucination of this Christ being. Making a real connection with the Christ being is no longer possible nowadays by merely reading the Gospels. All one gains by this means is a kind of subtle hallucination of Christ. This is why there is such a widespread theological view that the Christ did not indwell the man Jesus of Nazareth at all, but that the latter was just a historical individual like Socrates or Plato. The 'simple man from Nazareth' has in fact become the ideal of theologians. And very few of them of course know what to make of Paul's vision at Damascus—it is regarded as an hallucination since without spiritual-scientific insights people cannot come to a vision of the true Christ.

The Gospels have to be deepened through spiritual science. You see, drawing to the very greatest degree on the dullness that overcomes those who wish to live only within the narrow confines of their confessions, Ahriman will seek to reach his goal: that of overwhelming and stupefying humankind through his incarnation. Those who think they are the most Christian because they dismiss any further development of views about the Christ mystery are actually the ones who will most further Ahriman's ends through their pride and arrogance. The religious sects and confessions are a breeding ground for Ahriman. There is no use in deluding ourselves about these things. Just as Ahriman's cause is furthered by the materialistic outlook which dismisses everything spiritual and seeks to make a person into only what he eats and drinks, so his cause, not that of humanity, is furthered too by a rigid refusal of all spirit and a clinging to the literal words—the 'simple' view as people often say—of the Gospels.

You see, to prevent people becoming too narrowly constricted by an individual Gospel, the event of Golgotha is described from four different—only seemingly—contradictory perspectives in the four Gospels. This means that as long as people reflect just a little they will be protected from too literal a view. But in the sects which base everything on just one of the four Gospels—there are actually a good many of them—full rein is given to the seductive, dulling hallucinatory element that is induced by mere study of their words. At the time they were given, they had to act as a counterweight to the luciferic Gnosis. But if they are now taken as they were given they do not serve human progress but further the aims of Ahriman. Nothing is absolutely good in itself, but always only good or bad depending on what use is made of it. The best can be the worst if people do not use it in the right way. The loftiest qualities of the Gospel can have the most harmful effect if people are too self-satisfied to penetrate to a real, spiritual-scientific interpretation of these Gospels.

A great deal in the spiritual and unspiritual streams of today would necessitate people taking a clear view of it, and adapting their inner conduct accordingly. Whether or not human beings wish to penetrate these things with their understanding will dictate how Ahriman's incarnation affects them—whether it induces them to completely lose their earthly goal, or whether this incarnation of Ahriman can make them recognize that intellectual life alone, unspiritual life, is of very limited importance. If human beings take in hand, in the right way, what I described as streams leading inexorably towards Ahriman, then simply through the incarnation of Ahriman in earthly existence they will recognize clearly what is ahrimanic on the one hand as well as its polar opposite, the luciferic. And then, through discerning the contrast between the ahrimanic and the luciferic, they will become able inwardly to encompass the third, reconciling and combining element. Humankind needs to wrestle its way through to this trinity of Christ, Ahriman and Lucifer, for without this people of the future will not be able to progress in a way that can really fulfil their earthly goal.

Things connected with the science of the spirit can really only be properly understood if one takes them fully seriously. Spiritual science is not something that seeks to inform humanity today with some kind of sectarian spirit but is truly read from the needs of humanity's evolution. If we recognize these needs we cannot just choose to engage or not engage with it, but will see that all of human life, both physical and spiritual, must be illumined and pervaded by a spiritual-scientific perspective.

Just as there was once a luciferic incarnation in the East, and then a Christ incarnation at the midpoint as it were of world evolution, so an incarnation of Ahriman will take place in the West. This ahrimanic incarnation should not be avoided. It must come, for human beings have to look Ahriman squarely in the face, if you like. He will be the individuality who shows humankind the enormous shrewdness and acuity it can develop by calling on the earth forces that support and cultivate this acuity. In the distress and hardships I spoke of, that will come upon human beings in the near future, they will grow very inventive. Much will be discovered in the forces and substances of the world to provide food for human beings. But these discoveries will also show how matter is connected with the organs of reason—not of the spirit, but reason. People will learn what one must eat and drink to become very clever and astute. One cannot become spiritual through eating and drinking, but very astute and clever.

As yet people are unaware of such things. Rather than only seeking them, though, these things will arise by themselves through the hardships that will arise in the near future. By means of certain uses to which this knowledge will be put, secret societies that already exist and are making their preparations will pave the way for conditions that will enable the incarnation of Ahriman to occur on earth in the right way. And this incarnation should happen, for during our earthly evolution we ought also to recognize how much can emerge from purely material processes. At the same time, though, we must come to see how we can master the spiritual, or unspiritual, streams that lead us towards Ahriman.

When we realize that two conflicting political programmes can be proven to be equally beneficial, then we will understand that proof is not what is needed but a soul mood in which we experience living realities. What we experience in this way is different in kind from merely rational proof. Likewise we will realize that the Gospels must increasingly be deepened through spiritual science. Taking the Gospels literally, at face value, furthers ahrimanic culture. For purely external reasons we can understand that people today will no longer get anywhere by taking the Gospels literally. As you know, what is right for a particular period is no longer right for another. What is right at one time, becomes luciferic or ahrimanic at another. There was a time when reading the Gospels was enough. Today we must draw on the Gospels in a different way as we seek for spiritual knowledge of the Mystery of Golgotha.

Many people today certainly find it extremely uncomfortable to recognize such things. But if you have an interest in anthroposophy you should truly try to discern how strata of culture have gradually come to lie adjacent to each other, causing a chaos into which light must be shone once more.

One should try to read or listen to what some very radical modern person has to say about a particular issue of contemporary life, and compare it with the sermon, say, of a priest still wholly rooted in the mode of thinking and thought forms of older times. Then you really do find yourself confronted by two different worlds which you can only reconcile by avoiding clear-sighted scrutiny of the truth. Listen to a modern socialist speak about the social question, and then listen, say, to a Catholic spokesman on the same subject. It is very interesting to see how two distinct strata of culture live side by side, using words in quite different ways. A word used in one way by one of them has a quite different meaning for the other.

We should examine these things, illumine them with the light we can find if we give serious attention to reflections such as those we have sought to engage in today. In the end, people belonging to the positive religious confessions feel a kind of longing for religious deepening. It is by no means unimportant that such an outstanding mind, a positive Catholic spirit, such as Cardinal Newman, said when he was invested as cardinal in Rome that he saw no way forward for Christianity without a new revelation.[73]

Yes, Cardinal Newman said this: he could see no salvation for Christianity without a new revelation. But of course he did not have the courage to give serious credence to a new spiritual revelation. And the same is true of the others. There are countless pamphlets published today about what humanity needs, let us say in relation to social conditions. Another has just appeared, entitled *Socialism*, written by Robert Wilbrandt,[74] the son of the poet Wilbrandt.[75] In it he raises the social question, and clearly has a good foundation of detailed knowledge of the field. His conclusion is this: nothing will work without the spirit, and the course things are now taking shows this need for the spirit. But where does such a person get with this? He utters the word 'spirit', as an abstract concept, yet dismisses anything that really seeks to elaborate it. Digging around in abstractions, however much they go on about the spirit, is not yet spiritual. We ought not to confuse dull, abstract talk of spirit with the real, positive search for the content of the world of spirit—a search in which anthroposophically oriented spiritual science should engage.

Many people today speak about the spirit. But you who absorb spiritual science should refuse to allow yourselves to be fooled by mere talk of spirit. You should recognize that there is a difference between this vacuous talk and real accounts of the world of spirit as we seek to present them, based on anthroposophy. These describe the world of spirit in as real a way as the physical world of the senses can be outwardly described. You should be aware of the difference between the one and the other, repeatedly remembering that abstract talk of spirit is in fact a diversion from real spiritual enquiry, and that there are many people today who speak of the spirit but in doing so are distancing themselves ever further from it. Mere intellectual reference to the spirit does not lead to the spirit. What is intelligence in fact? What is the content of our human intelligence? I can explain this best to you if I offer the following picture. There are many ladies present who will perhaps understand this still better. Imagine that you are standing in front of a mirror and looking into it. This image of yourself that the mirror gives you is not in fact anything real but arises through the mirror's reflecting capacity. Now all that you possess inwardly as intelligence, as intellectual content, is also only a mirror image. There is no reality in it. And just as the mirror image of you is only produced by the mirror, so what is reflected in you as intelligence is only called forth by the physical instrument of your body, by your brain. Just as you cannot touch or stroke yourself if you reach towards your mirror image, so neither can you grasp the spirit if you turn only to the intellectual reflection, in which there is no spirit. What the intelligence grasps, however acute it is, never contains the spirit but only the picture of it. You cannot experience the spirit if you make do with mere intelligence; and the intelligence is so seductive because it offers a picture, a reflection of the spirit, but not the spirit itself. People think they do not need to make efforts to live their way into the spirit because they believe they already possess it, though all they possess is a reflection. To distinguish this—the mere image of the spirit from the real spirit—is the task of an outlook that goes beyond mere theorizing and seeks to dwell truly in a positive vision of the spirit.

That is what I wished to say to you today to reinforce the seriousness that should imbue our whole stance towards a life of the spirit grasped through anthroposophy. Our real onward evolution into the future will depend on how modern humanity regards this. If what I have described today is regarded as it is at present by most people, then Ahriman will be a terrible guest when he comes. But if people can find the will to take up into their awareness the things we have considered today, to govern and direct them so that humanity finds freedom in its stance towards the ahrimanic power, then when Ahriman appears humankind will learn exactly what it needs to through him: will see that though the earth must decline and decay, humanity by this very means can raise itself above earthly existence. After we reach a certain age in physical life, our physical body degenerates; and if we are sensible we do not complain about this, knowing that our soul is working its way towards a life that does not run parallel with this decline. In humanity lives something that is not one with the decline of the physical earth, which has already begun, but which will become ever more spiritual as the earth enters its physical decadence. Let us say this quite openly: the earth is growing

164 * Problems of Society

decadent, declining, as does human life in relation to its physical form. But by this very means let us find the strength to integrate into our civilization the immortal part of all earthly evolution that must emerge from humanity and live on as the earth moves towards its demise.

NOTES

Source texts

The transcripts of Lectures 1 to 4, and Lectures 9 and 10 were taken down in shorthand by Dornach stenographer Helene Finckh. For the third edition in 1977, the text of these lectures was reviewed and compared with the original shorthand transcripts. Changes from earlier editions originated then. Lectures 5 to 8 were recorded by Walter Vegelahn, but the original shorthand transcripts of these are not extant. For this 5th edition, the text was reviewed and edited, notes were corrected and extended.

1. The four lectures on 'The Social Question' were given in Zurich on 3, 5, 10 and 12 February 1919 see *Rudolf Steiner, The Social Question*, GA 328, and the book published the same year, *Towards Social Renewal*, GA 23.
2. At the Zschokke-Zweig, Zurich.
3. *The Soul's Probation*, Scene I. GA 14.
4. In his poem, 'Washing of the Feet', published in *Wir fanden einen Pfad*, 1914.
5. John 13:1–12.
6. See note 1: the public lecture of 3 February 1919.
7. Matthew 28:20.
8. Lectures in Bern on 6 and 7 February: 'The true shape of the social question, in response to the needs of contemporary humanity'; and 'Attempts to resolve social issues in the real ways that life requires'. These lectures are unpublished, but two lectures with the same title, of 3 and 5 February 1919, appeared in *The Social Question*, GA 328.
9. Lecture of 12 December 1918, in GA 186.
10. Luke 20:25.
11. Rudolf Steiner uses this expression in several lectures, indicating that this was used of Satan in esoteric Christianity. See also the lecture by Steiner on 20 April 1908 in Berlin, GA 102.
12. Lecture of 6 February 1919.
13. See Matthew 3:2.
14. See note 1.
15. See note 1, lecture of 12 February 1919.
16. The Great War, 1914–18.
17. See note 7.
18. See note 13.
19. In the lecture 'The work of the angel in our astral body', Zurich, 9 October 1918, and in 'How do I find the Christ?', Zurich 16 October 1918, GA 182.

20. Adolf von Harnack (1851–1930), leading Protestant ecclesiastical historian, Professor at Berlin University from 1889 to 1924, published 'The Nature of Christianity' (Leipzig 1900), 16 lectures to the students of all faculties given in 1899/1900 at Berlin University. The fourth edition of this book (Leipzig 1901), with handwritten notes and underlinings, is contained in Rudolf Steiner's library. Steiner often referred to Harnack in his lectures and in 1916–17 engaged particularly vociferously with him. See the lectures in Berlin, 16 May 1916, in GA 167; and on 14 August 1917 in GA 176.

21. Jean-Jacques Rousseau, 1712–78, Swiss-French philosopher. In relation to the theme Steiner raises here, see J.J. Rousseau, *Emile, or On Education*, 1762.

22. Matthew 25:40.

23. See note 1, lecture of 10 February 1919.

24. Epistle to the Galatians 2:20.

25. Kurt Eisner, 1867–1919, left-wing socialist politician of the 'Independent Socialist Party of Germany'. He was one of the leaders of the revolution in Munich in November 1918, and Prime Minister of Bavaria. On 21 February 1919 he was shot and killed by Count Anton Arco-Valley on his way to the opening of the regional parliament. Rudolf Steiner spoke to Eisner during the international conference of socialists on questions of war guilt, held in Bern between 3 and 10 February 1919, which Eisner attended as Bavarian Prime Minister (see Hans Kuehn, *Dreigliederungszeit*, Dornach 1987, pp. 33 f.).

26. Kurt Eisner, lecture on 'Socialism and Young People', given in Basel on 10 February 1919 at the invitation of Basel students. Published by the National-Zeitung, Basel 1919.

27. The first and third lectures of this volume.

28. Georg Friedrich Wilhelm Hegel, 1770–1831. In relation to Hegel's theory of the state, see especially his *Grundlinien der Philosophie des Rechts*, Berlin 1820 [*Elements of the Philosophy of Right*]. Rudolf Steiner comments further on this in his work *The Riddles of Philosophy*, GA 18.

29. Fritz Mauthner, 1849–1923, *Woerterbuch der Philosophie*, 1910–1911, the concept of 'res publica'. See also Rudolf Steiner's account of Mauthner and his Dictionary of Philosophy in the essay 'A new book on atheism' in the collected essays on the idea of the Goetheanum, GA 36.

30. For instance in Theobold von Bethmann Hollweg, *Betrachtungen zum Weltkrieg*, Part I, p. 62, Berlin 1919: a speech by the Foreign Minister Gottlieb von Jagow.

31. On 6 and 8–14 April 1914, in GA 153.

32. Vladimir Ilyich Lenin, 1870–1924.

33. Leo Trotsky, 1879–1940.

34. Johann Gottlieb Fichte, 1762–1814: *The Closed Commercial State*, 1800. See also Rudolf Steiner's comments in the lecture of 2 March 1919 in GA 189.

35. Ludwig Anzengruber, 1839–89, Austrian writer. *Ein Faustschlag*, play, Act 3, Scene 6: 'As true as God lives, I am an atheist!'

36. Vladimir Alexandrovich Sukhomlinov, Russian war minister at the outbreak of the First World War; see Sukhomlinov, *Die russische Mobilmachung im Lichte amtlicher Urkunden*, Bern 1917, p. 25. This book is in Rudolf Steiner's personal library.

37. Henrik Ibsen, 1818–1906, see among other works *The Enemy of the People*. See also Rudolf Steiner's comments on the occasion of Ibsen's seventieth birthday in *Das Magazin für Literatur*, in GA 32.
38. Bjørnstjerne Bjørnson, 1832–1910, Norwegian poet.
39. Gerhart Hauptmann, 1862–1945. *The Weavers*, 1892.
40. See Rudolf Steiner, essays on threefolding in GA 24: 'Preliminary remarks on "war guilt"'.
41. I Corinthians 3:19.
42. See note 40.
43. Karl Marx, 1818–83. *Capital*, 3 volumes published 1867, 1885 and 1894.
44. The November revolution of 1918/1919 at the end of the First World War led to the collapse of the monarchy in Germany and the establishing of a republican parliamentary democracy.
45. Premises of the Berlin branch of the Anthroposophical Society at Potsda-merstrasse 98. They were used from 1917. Prior to this the branch was located at Geisbergerstrasse 2, and before that originally at Motzstrasse 17.
46. *Education of the Human Race* by Gotthold Ephraim Lessing, 1729–81. See in particular Rudolf Steiner in *The Riddles of Philosophy*, GA 18.
47. On 7 September 1919. See GA 298.
48. *The Study of Man*, GA 293; *Practical Advice to Teachers*, GA 294; *Discussions with Teachers*, GA 295.
49. Lecture of 29 May 1917, in GA 176.
50. On 25 July 1919. More about this can be found in GA 337a [German edition] in the note to p. 96 on p. 328.
51. See note 44.
52. This may refer to Rudolf Steiner's lecture during the first study evening of the Association for the Threefold Social Organism, on 30 July 1919 in Stuttgart. There he discusses these themes in a very similar way. See GA 337a.
53. Lecture of 21 April 1919, in GA 192.
54. Galileo Galilei, 1564–1642; Copernicus, 1473–1543.
55. In the lecture of 12 September, during this same cycle of lectures, see p. 91.
56. Woodrow Wilson, 1856–1924, President of the United States during the First World War. See his speech dated 22 January 1917 at http://www.woodrowwilson.org/library-archives/wilson-elibrary. The book con-taining this speech was in Rudolf Steiner's library. See also Steiner's comments in the lecture of 11 March 1919, in GA 329.
57. Rabindranath Tagore, 1861–1941, Bengali lyric poet, author, composer, essayist and pedagogue. In 1913 Tagore was awarded the Nobel Prize for Literature. From 1912 he often travelled to Europe, America and East Asia, giving readings from his work and promoting Indian independence.
58. Lectures given in Kristiania (Oslo) between 7 and 17 June 1910, GA 121.
59. GA 9.
60. Gaius Caesar Germanicus, AD 12–41, Roman Caesar from AD 37 to 41.
61. See the essay on the threefold social organism in GA 24.
62. Erich Ludendorff, 1865–1937, German general during the First World War. See also Rudolf Steiner's comments on Ludendorff in the lectures of 23 and 24 November 1918, GA 185a.

63. Georg Michaelis, 1857–1936, German Chancellor from July to October 1917.

64. Goethe, *Maxims and Reflections*, 78.

65. See note 40.

66. Steiner is obliquely referring here to Goethe in *Faust* Part I, 'Night' verses 573–4.

67. See note 43.

68. See the public lecture series 'Social Future', six lectures given in October/November 1919 in Zurich: Lecture 2, 25 October 1919, GA 332a.

69. Steiner may here be referring to a passage in *The Transcendental Universe* by C.G. Harrison, London 1893. The preface states: 'When invested as Cardinal in Rome, Dr. Newman is said to have declared that he saw no hope for religion except through a new revelation.' Newman's actual words on 12 May 1879 in Rome were: 'Hitherto citizens have by and large been Christian. Even in countries separated from the Church as in my own—when I was young—the dictum held sway that Christianity was the law of the land. Today, this fine social system, which is the creation of Christianity, is laying aside Christianity everywhere. The dictum I referred to—along with a hundred others that followed from it—has vanished or is vanishing everywhere, and by the end of the century will have been forgotten, *unless the Almighty intervenes*!' (see Wilfrid Ward, *The Life of John Henry Cardinal Newman*, two vols., London 1927, vol. 2, pp. 460 f.).

70. *Lux Mundi*: 'A series of studies in the religion of the Incarnation. Edited by C. Gore, London 1913.' This was a collection of essays by various authors including one by Gore entitled 'The Holy Spirit and Inspiration!' Charles Gore (1853–1932) was an Anglican bishop and instigator of a modern trend within the High Church. This work is in Rudolf Steiner's library.

71. *The Apocalypse of St John*, 13 lectures in Nuremberg in June 1908, GA 104.

72. The Great War, 1914–18.

73. See note 69.

74. Robert Wilbrandt, 1875–1954, German economist. He attended the lecture by Rudolf Steiner on the threefold social organism on 2 June 1919 in Tuebingen, which was organized by a socialist student group. Wilbrandt later acted as supervisor for the first student dissertation on this theme (see also *Beitraege zur Rudolf Steiner Gesamtausgabe*, no. 103, Michaelmas 1989, p. 17). In his book *Sozialismus* (Jena 1919, p. 27), he wrote: 'Society is a spiritual body and relies on soul connections between people (this sentence is underlined in the copy in Rudolf Steiner's library). On page 118 he writes: 'This problem (making the spirit of Christianity into a reality) will only gradually be resolved within the inmost nature of humankind over centuries and millennia.' And on page 206: 'Socializing the economy is not enough. Education needs to be socialized too.'

75. Adolf von Wilbrandt, 1837–1911, German writer and director of Vienna's Burgtheater. Father of Robert Wilbrandt (see above).

RUDOLF STEINER'S COLLECTED WORKS

The German Edition of Rudolf Steiner's Collected Works (the *Gesamtausgabe* [GA] published by Rudolf Steiner Verlag, Dornach, Switzerland) presently runs to 354 titles, organized either by type of work (written or spoken), chronology, audience (public or other), or subject (education, art, etc.). For ease of comparison, the Collected Works in English [CW] follows the German organization exactly. A complete listing of the CWs follows with literal translations of the German titles. Other than in the case of the books published in his lifetime, titles were rarely given by Rudolf Steiner himself, and were often provided by the editors of the German editions. The titles in English are not necessarily the same as the German; and, indeed, over the past seventy-five years have frequently been different, with the same book sometimes appearing under different titles.

For ease of identification and to avoid confusion, we suggest that readers looking for a title should do so by CW number. Because the work of creating the Collected Works of Rudolf Steiner is an ongoing process, with new titles being published every year, we have not indicated in this listing which books are presently available. To find out what titles in the Collected Works are currently in print, please check our website at www.rudolfsteinerpress.com (or www.steinerbooks.org for US readers).

Written Work

Public Lectures

Lectures to the Members of the Anthroposophical Society

CW 88   Concerning the Astral World and Devachan
CW 89   Consciousness—Life—Form. Fundamental Principles of a Spiritual-Scientific Cosmology
CW 90   Participant Notes from the Lectures during the Years 1903–1905
CW 91   Participant Notes from the Lectures during the Years 1903–1905
CW 92   The Occult Truths of Ancient Myths and Sagas
CW 93   The Temple Legend and the Golden Legend
CW 93a   Fundamentals of Esotericism
CW 94   Cosmogony. Popular Occultism. The Gospel of John. The Theosophy in the Gospel of John
CW 95   At the Gates of Theosophy
CW 96   Origin-Impulses of Spiritual Science. Christian Esotericism in the Light of New Spirit-Knowledge
CW 97   The Christian Mystery
CW 98   Nature Beings and Spirit Beings—Their Effects in Our Visible World
CW 99   The Theosophy of the Rosicrucians
CW 100   Human Development and Christ-Knowledge
CW 101   Myths and Legends. Occult Signs and Symbols
CW 102   The Working into Human Beings by Spiritual Beings
CW 103   The Gospel of John
CW 104   The Apocalypse of John
CW 104a   From the Picture-Script of the Apocalypse of John
CW 105   Universe, Earth, the Human Being: Their Being and Development, as well as Their Reflection in the Connection between Egyptian Mythology and Modern Culture
CW 106   Egyptian Myths and Mysteries in Relation to the Active Spiritual Forces of the Present
CW 107   Spiritual-Scientific Knowledge of the Human Being
CW 108   Answering the Questions of Life and the World through Anthroposophy
CW 109   The Principle of Spiritual Economy in Connection with the Question of Reincarnation. An Aspect of the Spiritual Guidance of Humanity
CW 110   The Spiritual Hierarchies and Their Reflection in the Physical World. Zodiac, Planets and Cosmos
CW 111   Contained in CW 109
CW 112   The Gospel of John in Relation to the Three Other Gospels, Especially the Gospel of Luke
CW 113   The Orient in the Light of the Occident. The Children of Lucifer and the Brothers of Christ
CW 114   The Gospel of Luke
CW 115   Anthroposophy—Psychosophy—Pneumatosophy
CW 116   The Christ-Impulse and the Development of 'I'-Consciousness
CW 117   The Deeper Secrets of the Development of Humanity in Light of the Gospels

CW 291   The Nature of Colours
CW 291a   Knowledge of Colours. Supplementary Volume to 'The Nature of Colours'
CW 292   Art History as Image of Inner Spiritual Impulses
CW 293   General Knowledge of the Human Being as the Foundation of Pedagogy
CW 294   The Art of Education, Methodology and Didactics
CW 295   The Art of Education: Seminar Discussions and Lectures on Lesson Planning
CW 296   The Question of Education as a Social Question
CW 297   The Idea and Practice of the Waldorf School
CW 297a   Education for Life: Self-Education and the Practice of Pedagogy
CW 298   Rudolf Steiner in the Waldorf School
CW 299   Spiritual-Scientific Observations on Speech
CW 300a   Conferences with the Teachers of the Free Waldorf School in Stuttgart, 1919 to 1924, in 3 Volumes, Vol. 1
CW 300b   Conferences with the Teachers of the Free Waldorf School in Stuttgart, 1919 to 1924, in 3 Volumes, Vol. 2
CW 300c   Conferences with the Teachers of the Free Waldorf School in Stuttgart, 1919 to 1924, in 3 Volumes, Vol. 3
CW 301   The Renewal of Pedagogical-Didactical Art through Spiritual Science
CW 302   Knowledge of the Human Being and the Forming of Class Lessons
CW 302a   Education and Teaching from a Knowledge of the Human Being
CW 303   The Healthy Development of the Human Being
CW 304   Methods of Education and Teaching Based on Anthroposophy
CW 304a   Anthroposophical Knowledge of the Human Being and Pedagogy
CW 305   The Soul-Spiritual Foundational Forces of the Art of Education. Spiritual Values in Education and Social Life
CW 306   Pedagogical Praxis from the Viewpoint of a Spiritual-Scientific Knowledge of the Human Being. The Education of the Child and Young Human Beings
CW 307   The Spiritual Life of the Present and Education
CW 308   The Method of Teaching and the Life-Requirements for Teaching
CW 309   Anthroposophical Pedagogy and Its Prerequisites
CW 310   The Pedagogical Value of a Knowledge of the Human Being and the Cultural Value of Pedagogy
CW 311   The Art of Education from an Understanding of the Being of Humanity
CW 312   Spiritual Science and Medicine
CW 313   Spiritual-Scientific Viewpoints on Therapy
CW 314   Physiology and Therapy Based on Spiritual Science
CW 315   Curative Eurythmy
CW 316   Meditative Observations and Instructions for a Deepening of the Art of Healing
CW 317   The Curative Education Course

CW 342   Lectures and Courses on Christian Religious Work, Vol. 1: Anthroposophical Foundations for a Renewed Christian Religious Working

CW 343   Lectures and Courses on Christian Religious Work, Vol. 2: Spiritual Knowledge—Religious Feeling—Cultic Doing

CW 344   Lectures and Courses on Christian Religious Work, Vol. 3: Lectures at the Founding of the Christian Community

CW 345   Lectures and Courses on Christian Religious Work, Vol. 4: Concerning the Nature of the Working Word

CW 346   Lectures and Courses on Christian Religious Work, Vol. 5: The Apocalypse and the Work of the Priest

CW 347   The Knowledge of the Nature of the Human Being According to Body, Soul and Spirit. On Earlier Conditions of the Earth

CW 348   On Health and Illness. Foundations of a Spiritual-Scientific Doctrine of the Senses

CW 349   On the Life of the Human Being and of the Earth. On the Nature of Christianity

CW 350   Rhythms in the Cosmos and in the Human Being. How Does One Come To See the Spiritual World?

CW 351   The Human Being and the World. The Influence of the Spirit in Nature. On the Nature of Bees

CW 352   Nature and the Human Being Observed Spiritual-Scientifically

CW 353   The History of Humanity and the World-Views of the Folk Cultures

CW 354   The Creation of the World and the Human Being. Life on Earth and the Influence of the Stars

SIGNIFICANT EVENTS IN THE LIFE OF
RUDOLF STEINER

1829:   June 23: birth of Johann Steiner (1829–1910)—Rudolf Steiner's father—in Geras, Lower Austria.

1834:   May 8: birth of Franciska Blie (1834–1918)—Rudolf Steiner's mother—in Horn, Lower Austria. 'My father and mother were both children of the glorious Lower Austrian forest district north of the Danube.'

1860:   May 16: marriage of Johann Steiner and Franciska Blie.

1861:   February 25: birth of *Rudolf Joseph Lorenz Steiner* in Kraljevec, Croatia, near the border with Hungary, where Johann Steiner works as a telegrapher for the South Austria Railroad. Rudolf Steiner is baptized two days later, February 27, the date usually given as his birthday.

1862:   Summer: the family moves to Mödling, Lower Austria.

1863:   The family moves to Pottschach, Lower Austria, near the Styrian border, where Johann Steiner becomes stationmaster. 'The view stretched to the mountains ... majestic peaks in the distance and the sweet charm of nature in the immediate surroundings.'

1864:   November 15: birth of Rudolf Steiner's sister, Leopoldine (d. November 1, 1927). She will become a seamstress and live with her parents for the rest of her life.

1866:   July 28: birth of Rudolf Steiner's deaf-mute brother, Gustav (d. May 1, 1941).

1867:   Rudolf Steiner enters the village school. Following a disagreement between his father and the schoolmaster, whose wife falsely accused the boy of causing a commotion, Rudolf Steiner is taken out of school and taught at home.

1868:   A critical experience. Unknown to the family, an aunt dies in a distant town. Sitting in the station waiting room, Rudolf Steiner sees her 'form,' which speaks to him, asking for help. 'Beginning with this experience, a new soul life began in the boy, one in which not only the outer trees and mountains spoke to him, but also the worlds that lay behind them. From this moment on, the boy began to live with the spirits of nature ...'

1869:   The family moves to the peaceful, rural village of Neudörfl, near Wiener-Neustadt in present-day Austria. Rudolf Steiner attends the village school. Because of the 'unorthodoxy' of his writing and spelling, he has to do 'extra lessons.'

1870:   Through a book lent to him by his tutor, he discovers geometry: 'To grasp something purely in the spirit brought me inner happiness. I know that I first learned happiness through geometry.' The same tutor allows him to draw, while other students still struggle with their reading and writing. 'An artistic element' thus enters his education.

1871: Though his parents are not religious, Rudolf Steiner becomes a 'church child,' a favourite of the priest, who was 'an exceptional character.' 'Up to the age of ten or eleven, among those I came to know, he was far and away the most significant.' Among other things, he introduces Steiner to Copernican, heliocentric cosmology. As an altar boy, Rudolf Steiner serves at Masses, funerals, and Corpus Christi processions. At year's end, after an incident in which he escapes a thrashing, his father forbids him to go to church.

1872: Rudolf Steiner transfers to grammar school in Wiener-Neustadt, a five-mile walk from home, which must be done in all weathers.

1873–75: Through his teachers and on his own, Rudolf Steiner has many wonderful experiences with science and mathematics. Outside school, he teaches himself analytic geometry, trigonometry, differential equations, and calculus.

1876: Rudolf Steiner begins tutoring other students. He learns bookbinding from his father. He also teaches himself stenography.

1877: Rudolf Steiner discovers Kant's *Critique of Pure Reason*, which he reads and rereads. He also discovers and reads von Rotteck's *World History*.

1878: He studies extensively in contemporary psychology and philosophy.

1879: Rudolf Steiner graduates from high school with honours. His father is transferred to Inzersdorf, near Vienna. He uses his first visit to Vienna 'to purchase a great number of philosophy books'—Kant, Fichte, Schelling, and Hegel, as well as numerous histories of philosophy. His aim: to find a path from the 'I' to nature.

October 1879–1883: Rudolf Steiner attends the Technical College in Vienna—to study mathematics, chemistry, physics, mineralogy, botany, zoology, biology, geology, and mechanics—with a scholarship. He also attends lectures in history and literature, while avidly reading philosophy on his own. His two favourite professors are Karl Julius Schröer (German language and literature) and Edmund Reitlinger (physics). He also audits lectures by Robert Zimmermann on aesthetics and Franz Brentano on philosophy. During this year he begins his friendship with Moritz Zitter (1861–1921), who will help support him financially when he is in Berlin.

1880: Rudolf Steiner attends lectures on Schiller and Goethe by Karl Julius Schröer, who becomes his mentor. Also 'through a remarkable combination of circumstances,' he meets Felix Koguzki, a 'herb gatherer' and healer, who could 'see deeply into the secrets of nature.' Rudolf Steiner will meet and study with this 'emissary of the Master' throughout his time in Vienna.

1881: January: '... I didn't sleep a wink. I was busy with philosophical problems until about 12:30 a.m. Then, finally, I threw myself down on my couch. All my striving during the previous year had been to research whether the following statement by Schelling was true or not: *Within everyone dwells a secret, marvelous capacity to draw back from the stream of time—out of the self clothed in all that comes to us from outside—into our innermost being and there, in the immutable form of the Eternal, to look into ourselves.* I believe, and I am still quite certain of it, that I discovered this capacity in myself; I had long had an inkling of it. Now the whole of idealist philosophy stood before me in modified form. What's a sleepless night compared to that!'

Rudolf Steiner begins communicating with leading thinkers of the day, who send him books in return, which he reads eagerly.

July: 'I am not one of those who dives into the day like an animal in human form. I pursue a quite specific goal, an idealistic aim—knowledge of the truth! This cannot be done offhandedly. It requires the greatest striving in the world, free of all egotism, and equally of all resignation.'

August: Steiner puts down on paper for the first time thoughts for a 'Philosophy of Freedom.' 'The striving for the absolute: this human yearning is freedom.' He also seeks to outline a 'peasant philosophy,' describing what the worldview of a 'peasant'—one who lives close to the earth and the old ways—really is.

1881–1882: Felix Koguzki, the herb gatherer, reveals himself to be the envoy of another, higher initiatory personality, who instructs Rudolf Steiner to penetrate Fichte's philosophy and to master modern scientific thinking as a preparation for right entry into the spirit. This 'Master' also teaches him the double (evolutionary and involutionary) nature of time.

1882:   Through the offices of Karl Julius Schröer, Rudolf Steiner is asked by Joseph Kürschner to edit Goethe's scientific works for the *Deutschen National-Literatur* edition. He writes 'A Possible Critique of Atomistic Concepts' and sends it to Friedrich Theodor Vischer.

1883:   Rudolf Steiner completes his college studies and begins work on the Goethe project.

1884:   First volume of Goethe's *Scientific Writings* (CW 1) appears (March). He lectures on Goethe and Lessing, and Goethe's approach to science. In July, he enters the household of Ladislaus and Pauline Specht as tutor to the four Specht boys. He will live there until 1890. At this time, he meets Josef Breuer (1842–1925), the co-author with Sigmund Freud of *Studies in Hysteria*, who is the Specht family doctor.

1885:   While continuing to edit Goethe's writings, Rudolf Steiner reads deeply in contemporary philosophy (Eduard von Hartmann, Johannes Volkelt, and Richard Wahle, among others).

1886:   May: Rudolf Steiner sends Kürschner the manuscript of *Outlines of Goethe's Theory of Knowledge* (CW 2), which appears in October, and which he sends out widely. He also meets the poet Marie Eugenie Delle Grazie and writes 'Nature and Our Ideals' for her. He attends her salon, where he meets many priests, theologians, and philosophers, who will become his friends. Meanwhile, the director of the Goethe Archive in Weimar requests his collaboration with the *Sophien* edition of Goethe's works, particularly the writings on colour.

1887:   At the beginning of the year, Rudolf Steiner is very sick. As the year progresses and his health improves, he becomes increasingly 'a man of letters,' lecturing, writing essays, and taking part in Austrian cultural life. In August–September, the second volume of Goethe's *Scientific Writings* appears.

1888: January–July: Rudolf Steiner assumes editorship of the 'German Weekly' (*Deutsche Wochenschrift*). He begins lecturing more intensively, giving, for example, a lecture titled 'Goethe as Father of a New Aesthetics.' He meets and becomes soul friends with Friedrich Eckstein (1861–1939), a vegetarian, philosopher of symbolism, alchemist, and musician, who will introduce him to various spiritual currents (including Theosophy) and with whom he will meditate and interpret esoteric and alchemical texts.

1889: Rudolf Steiner first reads Nietzsche (*Beyond Good and Evil*). He encounters Theosophy again and learns of Madame Blavatsky in the Theosophical circle around Marie Lang (1858–1934). Here he also meets well-known figures of Austrian life, as well as esoteric figures like the occultist Franz Hartmann and Karl Leinigen-Billigen (translator of C.G. Harrison's *The Transcendental Universe*). During this period, Steiner first reads A.P. Sinnett's *Esoteric Buddhism* and Mabel Collins's *Light on the Path*. He also begins travelling, visiting Budapest, Weimar, and Berlin (where he meets philosopher Eduard von Hartmann).

1890: Rudolf Steiner finishes volume 3 of Goethe's scientific writings. He begins his doctoral dissertation, which will become *Truth and Science* (CW 3). He also meets the poet and feminist Rosa Mayreder (1858–1938), with whom he can exchange his most intimate thoughts. In September, Rudolf Steiner moves to Weimar to work in the Goethe-Schiller Archive.

1891: Volume 3 of the Kürschner edition of Goethe appears. Meanwhile, Rudolf Steiner edits Goethe's studies in mineralogy and scientific writings for the *Sophien* edition. He meets Ludwig Laistner of the Cotta Publishing Company, who asks for a book on the basic question of metaphysics. From this will result, ultimately, *The Philosophy of Freedom* (CW 4), which will be published not by Cotta but by Emil Felber. In October, Rudolf Steiner takes the oral exam for a doctorate in philosophy, mathematics, and mechanics at Rostock University, receiving his doctorate on the twenty-sixth. In November, he gives his first lecture on Goethe's 'Fairy Tale' in Vienna.

1892: Rudolf Steiner continues work at the Goethe-Schiller Archive and on his *Philosophy of Freedom*. *Truth and Science*, his doctoral dissertation, is published. Steiner undertakes to write introductions to books on Schopenhauer and Jean Paul for Cotta. At year's end, he finds lodging with Anna Eunike, née Schulz (1853–1911), a widow with four daughters and a son. He also develops a friendship with Otto Erich Hartleben (1864–1905) with whom he shares literary interests.

1893: Rudolf Steiner begins his habit of producing many reviews and articles. In March, he gives a lecture titled 'Hypnotism, with Reference to Spiritism.' In September, volume 4 of the Kürschner edition is completed. In November, *The Philosophy of Freedom* appears. This year, too, he meets John Henry Mackay (1864–1933), the anarchist, and Max Stirner, a scholar and biographer.

1894: Rudolf Steiner meets Elisabeth Förster Nietzsche, the philosopher's sister, and begins to read Nietzsche in earnest, beginning with the as yet unpublished *Antichrist*. He also meets Ernst Haeckel (1834–1919). In the fall, he begins to write *Nietzsche, A Fighter against His Time* (CW 5).

1895:   May, *Nietzsche, A Fighter against His Time* appears.

1896:   January 22: Rudolf Steiner sees Friedrich Nietzsche for the first and only time. Moves between the Nietzsche and the Goethe-Schiller Archives, where he completes his work before year's end. He falls out with Elisabeth Förster Nietzsche, thus ending his association with the Nietzsche Archive.

1897:   Rudolf Steiner finishes the manuscript of *Goethe's Worldview* (CW 6). He moves to Berlin with Anna Eunike and begins editorship of the *Magazin für Literatur*. From now on, Steiner will write countless reviews, literary and philosophical articles, and so on. He begins lecturing at the 'Free Literary Society.' In September, he attends the Zionist Congress in Basel. He sides with Dreyfus in the Dreyfus affair.

1898:   Rudolf Steiner is very active as an editor in the political, artistic, and theatrical life of Berlin. He becomes friendly with John Henry Mackay and poet Ludwig Jacobowski (1868–1900). He joins Jacobowski's circle of writers, artists, and scientists—'The Coming Ones' (*Die Kommenden*)— and contributes lectures to the group until 1903. He also lectures at the 'League for College Pedagogy.' He writes an article for Goethe's sesquicentennial, 'Goethe's Secret Revelation,' on the 'Fairy Tale of the Green Snake and the Beautiful Lily.'

1898–99: 'This was a trying time for my soul as I looked at Christianity. . . . I was able to progress only by contemplating, by means of spiritual perception, the evolution of Christianity. . . . Conscious knowledge of real Christianity began to dawn in me around the turn of the century. This seed continued to develop. My soul trial occurred shortly before the beginning of the twentieth century. It was decisive for my soul's development that I stood spiritually before the Mystery of Golgotha in a deep and solemn celebration of knowledge.'

1899:   Rudolf Steiner begins teaching and giving lectures and lecture cycles at the Workers' College, founded by Wilhelm Liebknecht (1826–1900). He will continue to do so until 1904. Writes: *Literature and Spiritual Life in the Nineteenth Century; Individualism in Philosophy; Haeckel and His Opponents; Poetry in the Present;* and begins what will become (fifteen years later) *The Riddles of Philosophy* (CW 18). He also meets many artists and writers, including Käthe Kollwitz, Stefan Zweig, and Rainer Maria Rilke. On October 31, he marries Anna Eunike.

1900:   'I thought that the turn of the century must bring humanity a new light. It seemed to me that the separation of human thinking and willing from the spirit had peaked. A turn or reversal of direction in human evolution seemed to me a necessity.' Rudolf Steiner finishes *World and Life Views in the Nineteenth Century* (the second part of what will become *The Riddles of Philosophy*) and dedicates it to Ernst Haeckel. It is published in March. He continues lecturing at *Die Kommenden*, whose leadership he assumes after the death of Jacobowski. Also, he gives the Gutenberg Jubilee lecture before 7,000 typesetters and printers. In September, Rudolf Steiner is invited by Count and Countess Brockdorff to lecture in the Theosophical Library. His first lecture is on Nietzsche. His second lecture is titled 'Goethe's Secret Revelation.' October 6, he begins a lecture cycle on the mystics that will become *Mystics after Modernism* (CW 7). November–December: 'Marie von Sivers appears in the audience....' Also in November, Steiner gives his first lecture at the Giordano Bruno Bund (where he will continue to lecture until May, 1905). He speaks on Bruno and modern Rome, focusing on the importance of the philosophy of Thomas Aquinas as monism.

1901:   In continual financial straits, Rudolf Steiner's early friends Moritz Zitter and Rosa Mayreder help support him. In October, he begins the lecture cycle *Christianity as Mystical Fact* (CW 8) at the Theosophical Library. In November, he gives his first 'Theosophical lecture' on Goethe's 'Fairy Tale' in Hamburg at the invitation of Wilhelm Hubbe-Schleiden. He also attends a gathering to celebrate the founding of the Theosophical Society at Count and Countess Brockdorff's. He gives a lecture cycle, 'From Buddha to Christ,' for the circle of the *Kommenden*. November 17, Marie von Sivers asks Rudolf Steiner if Theosophy needs a Western-Christian spiritual movement (to complement Theosophy's Eastern emphasis). 'The question was posed. Now, following spiritual laws, I could begin to give an answer....' In December, Rudolf Steiner writes his first article for a Theosophical publication. At year's end, the Brockdorffs and possibly Wilhelm Hubbe-Schleiden ask Rudolf Steiner to join the Theosophical Society and undertake the leadership of the German section. Rudolf Steiner agrees, on the condition that Marie von Sivers (then in Italy) work with him.

1902:   Beginning in January, Rudolf Steiner attends the opening of the Workers' School in Spandau with Rosa Luxemburg (1870–1919). January 17, Rudolf Steiner joins the Theosophical Society. In April, he is asked to become general secretary of the German Section of the Theosophical Society, and works on preparations for its founding. In July, he visits London for a Theosophical congress. He meets Bertram Keightly, G.R.S. Mead, A.P. Sinnett, and Annie Besant, among others. In September, *Christianity as Mystical Fact* appears. In October, Rudolf Steiner gives his first public lecture on Theosophy ('Monism and Theosophy') to about three hundred people at the Giordano Bruno Bund. On October 19–21, the German Section of the Theosophical Society has its first meeting; Rudolf Steiner is the general secretary, and Annie Besant attends. Steiner lectures on practical karma studies. On October 23, Annie Besant inducts Rudolf Steiner into the Esoteric School of the Theosophical Society. On October 25, Steiner begins a weekly series of lectures: 'The Field of Theosophy.' During this year, Rudolf Steiner also first meets Ita Wegman (1876–1943), who will become his close collaborator in his final years.

1903:   Rudolf Steiner holds about 300 lectures and seminars. In May, the first issue of the periodical *Luzifer* appears. In June, Rudolf Steiner visits

London for the first meeting of the Federation of the European Sections of the Theosophical Society, where he meets Colonel Olcott. He begins to write *Theosophy* (CW 9).

1904:   Rudolf Steiner continues lecturing at the Workers' College and elsewhere (about 90 lectures), while lecturing intensively all over Germany among Theosophists (about 140 lectures). In February, he meets Carl Unger (1878–1929), who will become a member of the board of the Anthroposophical Society (1913). In March, he meets Michael Bauer (1871–1929), a Christian mystic, who will also be on the board. In May, *Theosophy* appears, with the dedication: 'To the spirit of Giordano Bruno.' Rudolf Steiner and Marie von Sivers visit London for meetings with Annie Besant. June: Rudolf Steiner and Marie von Sivers attend the meeting of the Federation of European Sections of the Theosophical Society in Amsterdam. In July, Steiner begins the articles in *Luzifer-Gnosis* that will become *How to Know Higher Worlds* (CW 10) and *Cosmic Memory* (CW 11). In September, Annie Besant visits Germany. In December, Steiner lectures on Freemasonry. He mentions the High Grade Masonry derived from John Yarker and represented by Theodore Reuss and Karl Kellner as a blank slate 'into which a good image could be placed.'

1905:   This year, Steiner ends his non-Theosophical lecturing activity. Supported by Marie von Sivers, his Theosophical lecturing—both in public and in the Theosophical Society—increases significantly: 'The German Theosophical Movement is of exceptional importance.' Steiner recommends reading, among others, Fichte, Jacob Boehme, and Angelus Silesius. He begins to introduce Christian themes into Theosophy. He also begins to work with doctors (Felix Peipers and Ludwig Noll). In July, he is in London for the Federation of European Sections, where he attends a lecture by Annie Besant: 'I have seldom seen Mrs. Besant speak in so inward and heartfelt a manner....' 'Through Mrs. Besant I have found the way to H.P. Blavatsky.' September to October, he gives a course of thirty-one lectures for a small group of esoteric students. In October, the annual meeting of the German Section of the Theosophical Society, which still remains very small, takes place. Rudolf Steiner reports membership has risen from 121 to 377 members. In November, seeking to establish esoteric 'continuity,' Rudolf Steiner and Marie von Sivers participate in a 'Memphis-Misraim' Masonic ceremony. They pay forty-five marks for membership. 'Yesterday, you saw how little remains of former esoteric institutions.' 'We are dealing only with a "framework"... for the present, nothing lies behind it. The occult powers have completely withdrawn.'

1906:   Expansion of Theosophical work. Rudolf Steiner gives about 245 lectures, only 44 of which take place in Berlin. Cycles are given in Paris, Leipzig, Stuttgart, and Munich. Esoteric work also intensifies. Rudolf Steiner begins writing *An Outline of Esoteric Science* (CW 13). In January, Rudolf Steiner receives permission (a patent) from the Great Orient of the Scottish A & A Thirty-Three Degree Rite of the Order of the Ancient

Freemasons of the Memphis-Misraim Rite to direct a chapter under the name 'Mystica Aeterna.' This will become the 'Cognitive-Ritual Section' (also called 'Misraim Service') of the Esoteric School. (See: *Freemasonry and Ritual Work: The Misraim Service*, CW 265). During this time, Steiner also meets Albert Schweitzer. In May, he is in Paris, where he visits Edouard Schuré. Many Russians attend his lectures (including Konstantin Balmont, Dimitri Mereszkovski, Zinaida Hippius, and Maximilian Woloshin). He attends the General Meeting of the European Federation of the Theosophical Society, at which Col. Olcott is present for the last time. He spends the year's end in Venice and Rome, where he writes and works on his translation of H.P. Blavatsky's *Key to Theosophy*.

1907:   Further expansion of the German Theosophical Movement according to the Rosicrucian directive to 'introduce spirit into the world'—in education, in social questions, in art, and in science. In February, Col. Olcott dies in Adyar. Before he dies, Olcott indicates that 'the Masters' wish Annie Besant to succeed him: much politicking ensues. Rudolf Steiner supports Besant's candidacy. April-May: preparations for the Congress of the Federation of European Sections of the Theosophical Society—the great, watershed Whitsun 'Munich Congress,' attended by Annie Besant and others. Steiner decides to separate Eastern and Western (Christian-Rosicrucian) esoteric schools. He takes his esoteric school out of the Theosophical Society (Besant and Rudolf Steiner are 'in harmony' on this). Steiner makes his first lecture tours to Austria and Hungary. That summer, he is in Italy. In September, he visits Edouard Schuré, who will write the introduction to the French edition of *Christianity as Mystical Fact* in Barr, Alsace. Rudolf Steiner writes the autobiographical statement known as the 'Barr Document.' In *Luzifer-Gnosis*, 'The Education of the Child' appears.

1908:   The movement grows (membership: 1,150). Lecturing expands. Steiner makes his first extended lecture tour to Holland and Scandinavia, as well as visits to Naples and Sicily. Themes: St. John's Gospel, the Apocalypse, Egypt, science, philosophy, and logic. *Luzifer-Gnosis* ceases publication. In Berlin, Marie von Sivers (with Johanna Mücke (1864–1949) forms the *Philosophisch-Theosophisch* (after 1915 *Philosophisch-Anthroposophisch*) *Verlag* to publish Steiner's work. Steiner gives lecture cycles titled *The Gospel of St. John* (CW 103) and *The Apocalypse* (104).

1909:   *An Outline of Esoteric Science* appears. Lecturing and travel continues. Rudolf Steiner's spiritual research expands to include the polarity of Lucifer and Ahriman; the work of great individualities in history; the Maitreya Buddha and the Bodhisattvas; spiritual economy (CW 109); the work of the spiritual hierarchies in heaven and on earth (CW 110). He also deepens and intensifies his research into the Gospels, giving lectures on the Gospel of St. Luke (CW 114) with the first mention of two Jesus children. Meets and becomes friends with Christian Morgenstern (1871–1914). In April, he lays the foundation stone for the Malsch model—the building that will lead to the first Goetheanum. In May, the International Congress of the Federation of European Sections of the

Theosophical Society takes place in Budapest. Rudolf Steiner receives the Subba Row medal for *How to Know Higher Worlds*. During this time, Charles W. Leadbeater discovers Jiddu Krishnamurti (1895–1986) and proclaims him the future 'world teacher,' the bearer of the Maitreya Buddha and the 'reappearing Christ.' In October, Steiner delivers seminal lectures on 'anthroposophy,' which he will try, unsuccessfully, to rework over the next years into the unfinished work, *Anthroposophy (A Fragment)* (CW 45).

1910:   New themes: *The Reappearance of Christ in the Etheric* (CW 118); *The Fifth Gospel; The Mission of Folk Souls* (CW 121); *Occult History* (CW 126); the evolving development of etheric cognitive capacities. Rudolf Steiner continues his Gospel research with *The Gospel of St. Matthew* (CW 123). In January, his father dies. In April, he takes a month-long trip to Italy, including Rome, Monte Cassino, and Sicily. He also visits Scandinavia again. July–August, he writes the first mystery drama, *The Portal of Initiation* (CW 14). In November, he gives 'psychosophy' lectures. In December, he submits 'On the Psychological Foundations and Episte-mological Framework of Theosophy' to the International Philosophical Congress in Bologna.

1911:   The crisis in the Theosophical Society deepens. In January, 'The Order of the Rising Sun,' which will soon become 'The Order of the Star in the East,' is founded for the coming world teacher, Krishnamurti. At the same time, Marie von Sivers, Rudolf Steiner's co-worker, falls ill. Fewer lectures are given, but important new ground is broken. In Prague, in March, Steiner meets Franz Kafka (1883–1924) and Hugo Bergmann (1883-1975). In April, he delivers his paper to the Philosophical Con-gress. He writes the second mystery drama, *The Soul's Probation* (CW 14). Also, while Marie von Sivers is convalescing, Rudolf Steiner begins work on *Calendar 1912/1913*, which will contain the 'Calendar of the Soul' meditations. On March 19, Anna (Eunike) Steiner dies. In September, Rudolf Steiner visits Einsiedeln, birthplace of Paracelsus. In December, Friedrich Rittelmeyer, future founder of the Christian Community, meets Rudolf Steiner. The *Johannes-Bauverein*, the 'building committee,' which would lead to the first Goetheanum (first planned for Munich), is also founded, and a preliminary committee for the founding of an indepen-dent association is created that, in the following year, will become the Anthroposophical Society. Important lecture cycles include *Occult Phy-siology* (CW 128); *Wonders of the World* (CW 129); *From Jesus to Christ* (CW 131). Other themes: esoteric Christianity; Christian Rosenkreutz; the spiritual guidance of humanity; the sense world and the world of the spirit.

1912:   Despite the ongoing, now increasing crisis in the Theosophical Society, much is accomplished: *Calendar 1912/1913* is published; eurythmy is created; both the third mystery drama, *The Guardian of the Threshold* (CW 14) and *A Way of Self-Knowledge* (CW 16) are written. New (or renewed) themes included life between death and rebirth and karma and reincarnation. Other lecture cycles: *Spiritual Beings in the Heavenly Bodies and in the Kingdoms of Nature* (CW 136); *The Human Being in the Light of Occultism, Theosophy, and Philosophy* (CW 137); *The Gospel of St. Mark* (CW 139); and *The Bhagavad Gita and the Epistles of Paul* (CW 142). On May 8, Rudolf Steiner celebrates White Lotus Day, H.P. Blavatsky's death day, which he had faithfully observed for the past decade, for the last time. In August, Rudolf Steiner suggests the 'independent association' be called the 'Anthroposophical Society.' In September, the first eurythmy course takes place. In October, Rudolf Steiner declines recognition of a Theosophical Society lodge dedicated to the Star of the East and decides to expel all Theosophical Society members belonging to the order. Also, with Marie von Sivers, he first visits Dornach, near Basel, Switzerland, and they stand on the hill where the Goetheanum will be built. In November, a Theosophical Society lodge is opened by direct mandate from Adyar (Annie Besant). In December, a meeting of the German section occurs at which it is decided that belonging to the Order of the Star of the East is incompatible with membership in the Theosophical Society. December 28: informal founding of the Anthroposophical Society in Berlin.

1913:　Expulsion of the German section from the Theosophical Society. February 2–3: Foundation meeting of the Anthroposophical Society. Board members include: Marie von Sivers, Michael Bauer, and Carl Unger. September 20: Laying of the foundation stone for the *Johannes Bau* (Goetheanum) in Dornach. Building begins immediately. The third mystery drama, *The Soul's Awakening* (CW 14), is completed. Also: *The Threshold of the Spiritual World* (CW 147). Lecture cycles include: *The Bhagavad Gita and the Epistles of Paul* and *The Esoteric Meaning of the Bhagavad Gita* (CW 146), which the Russian philosopher Nikolai Berdyaev attends; *The Mysteries of the East and of Christianity* (CW 144); *The Effects of Esoteric Development* (CW 145); and *The Fifth Gospel* (CW 148). In May, Rudolf Steiner is in London and Paris, where anthroposophical work continues.

1914:　Building continues on the *Johannes Bau* (Goetheanum) in Dornach, with artists and co-workers from seventeen nations. The general assembly of the Anthroposophical Society takes place. In May, Rudolf Steiner visits Paris, as well as Chartres Cathedral. June 28: assassination in Sarajevo ('Now the catastrophe has happened!'). August 1: War is declared. Rudolf Steiner returns to Germany from Dornach—he will travel back and forth. He writes the last chapter of *The Riddles of Philosophy*. Lecture cycles include: *Human and Cosmic Thought* (CW 151); *Inner Being of Humanity between Death and a New Birth* (CW 153); *Occult Reading and Occult Hearing* (CW 156). December 24: marriage of Rudolf Steiner and Marie von Sivers.

1915:　Building continues. Life after death becomes a major theme, also art. Writes: *Thoughts during a Time of War* (CW 24). Lectures include: *The Secret of Death* (CW 159); *The Uniting of Humanity through the Christ Impulse* (CW 165).

1916:　Rudolf Steiner begins work with Edith Maryon (1872–1924) on the sculpture 'The Representative of Humanity' ('The Group'—Christ, Lucifer, and Ahriman). He also works with the alchemist Alexander von Bernus on the quarterly *Das Reich*. He writes *The Riddle of Humanity* (CW 20). Lectures include: *Necessity and Freedom in World History and Human Action* (CW 166); *Past and Present in the Human Spirit* (CW 167); *The Karma of Vocation* (CW 172); *The Karma of Untruthfulness* (CW 173).

1917:   Russian Revolution. The U.S. enters the war. Building continues. Rudolf Steiner delineates the idea of the 'threefold nature of the human being' (in a public lecture March 15) and the 'threefold nature of the social organism' (hammered out in May-June with the help of Otto von Lerchenfeld and Ludwig Polzer-Hoditz in the form of two documents titled *Memoranda*, which were distributed in high places). August–September: Rudolf Steiner writes *The Riddles of the Soul* (CW 20). Also: commentary on 'The Chymical Wedding of Christian Rosenkreutz' for Alexander Bernus (*Das Reich*). Lectures include: *The Karma of Materialism* (CW 176); *The Spiritual Background of the Outer World: The Fall of the Spirits of Darkness* (CW 177).

1918:   March 18: peace treaty of Brest-Litovsk—'Now everything will truly enter chaos! What is needed is cultural renewal.' June: Rudolf Steiner visits Karlstein (Grail) Castle outside Prague. Lecture cycle: *From Symptom to Reality in Modern History* (CW 185). In mid-November, Emil Molt, of the Waldorf-Astoria Cigarette Company, has the idea of founding a school for his workers' children.

1919:   Focus on the threefold social organism: tireless travel, countless lectures, meetings, and publications. At the same time, a new public stage of Anthroposophy emerges as cultural renewal begins. The coming years will see initiatives in pedagogy, medicine, pharmacology, and agriculture. January 27: threefold meeting: ' We must first of all, with the money we have, found free schools that can bring people what they need.' February: first public eurythmy performance in Zurich. Also: 'Appeal to the German People' (CW 24), circulated March 6 as a newspaper insert. In April, *Towards Social Renewal* (CW 23) appears—'perhaps the most widely read of all books on politics appearing since the war.' Rudolf Steiner is asked to undertake the 'direction and leadership' of the school founded by the Waldorf-Astoria Company. Rudolf Steiner begins to talk about the 'renewal' of education. May 30: a building is selected and purchased for the future Waldorf School. August–September, Rudolf Steiner gives a lecture course for Waldorf teachers, *The Foundations of Human Experience (Study of Man)* (CW 293). September 7: Opening of the first Waldorf School. December (into January): first science course, the *Light Course* (CW 320).

1920:   The Waldorf School flourishes. New threefold initiatives. Founding of limited companies *Der Kommende Tag* and *Futurum A.G.* to infuse spiritual values into the economic realm. Rudolf Steiner also focuses on the sciences. Lectures: *Introducing Anthroposophical Medicine* (CW 312); *The Warmth Course* (CW 321); *The Boundaries of Natural Science* (CW 322); *The Redemption of Thinking* (CW 74). February: Johannes Werner

Klein—later a co-founder of the Christian Community—asks Rudolf Steiner about the possibility of a 'religious renewal,' a 'Johannine church.' In March, Rudolf Steiner gives the first course for doctors and medical students. In April, a divinity student asks Rudolf Steiner a second time about the possibility of religious renewal. September 27–October 16: anthroposophical 'university course.' December: lectures titled *The Search for the New Isis* (CW 202).

1921: Rudolf Steiner continues his intensive work on cultural renewal, including the uphill battle for the threefold social order. 'University' arts, scientific, theological, and medical courses include: *The Astronomy Course* (CW 323); *Observation, Mathematics, and Scientific Experiment* (CW 324); the *Second Medical Course* (CW 313); *Colour*. In June and September-October, Rudolf Steiner also gives the first two 'priests' courses' (CW 342 and 343). The 'youth movement' gains momentum. Magazines are founded: *Die Drei* (January), and—under the editorship of Albert Steffen (1884–1963)—the weekly, *Das Goetheanum* (August). In February–March, Rudolf Steiner takes his first trip outside Germany since the war (Holland). On April 7, Steiner receives a letter regarding 'religious renewal,' and May 22–23, he agrees to address the question in a practical way. In June, the Klinical-Therapeutic Institute opens in Arlesheim under the direction of Dr. Ita Wegman. In August, the Chemical-Pharmaceutical Laboratory opens in Arlesheim (Oskar Schmiedel and Ita Wegman are directors). The Clinical Therapeutic Institute is inaugurated in Stuttgart (Dr. Ludwig Noll is director); also the Research Laboratory in Dornach (Ehrenfried Pfeiffer and Günther Wachsmuth are directors). In November–December, Rudolf Steiner visits Norway.

1922: The first half of the year involves very active public lecturing (thousands attend); in the second half, Rudolf Steiner begins to withdraw and turn toward the Society—'The Society is asleep.' It is 'too weak' to do what is asked of it. The businesses—*Der Kommende Tag* and *Futurum A.G.*—fail. In January, with the help of an agent, Steiner undertakes a twelve-city German lecture tour, accompanied by eurythmy performances. In two weeks he speaks to more than 2,000 people. In April, he gives a 'university course' in The Hague. He also visits England. In June, he is in Vienna for the East–West Congress. In August–September, he is back in England for the Oxford Conference on Education. Returning to Dornach, he gives the lectures *Philosophy, Cosmology, and Religion* (CW 215), and gives the third priests' course (CW 344). On September 16, The Christian Community is founded. In October–November, Steiner is in Holland and England. He also speaks to the youth: *The Youth Course* (CW 217). In December, Steiner gives lectures titled *The Origins of Natural Science* (CW 326), and *Humanity and the World of Stars: The Spiritual Communion of Humanity* (CW 219). December 31: Fire at the Goetheanum, which is destroyed.

1923: Despite the fire, Rudolf Steiner continues his work unabated. A very hard year. Internal dispersion, dissension, and apathy abound. There is conflict—between old and new visions—within the Society. A wake-up call is needed, and Rudolf Steiner responds with renewed lecturing vitality. His focus: the spiritual context of human life; initiation science; the course of the year; and community building. As a foundation for an artistic school, he creates a series of pastel sketches. Lecture cycles: *The Anthroposophical Movement; Initiation Science* (CW 227) (in England at the Penmaenmawr Summer School); *The Four Seasons and the Archangels* (CW 229); *Harmony of the Creative Word* (CW 230); *The Supersensible Human* (CW 231), given in Holland for the founding of the Dutch society. On November 10, in response to the failed Hitler-Ludendorff putsch in Munich, Steiner closes his Berlin residence and moves the *Philosophisch-Anthroposophisch Verlag* (Press) to Dornach. On December 9, Steiner begins the serialization of his *Autobiography: The Course of My Life* (CW 28) in *Das Goetheanum*. It will continue to appear weekly, without a break, until his death. Late December–early January: Rudolf Steiner re-founds the Anthroposophical Society (about 12,000 members internationally) and takes over its leadership. The new board members are: Marie Steiner, Ita Wegman, Albert Steffen, Elisabeth Vreede, and Günther Wachsmuth. (See *The Christmas Meeting for the Founding of the General Anthroposophical Society*, CW 260). Accompanying lectures: *Mystery Knowledge and Mystery Centres* (CW 232); *World History in the Light of Anthroposophy* (CW 233). December 25: the Foundation Stone is laid (in the hearts of members) in the form of the 'Foundation Stone Meditation.'

1924:   January 1: having founded the Anthroposophical Society and taken over its leadership, Rudolf Steiner has the task of 'reforming' it. The process begins with a weekly newssheet ('What's Happening in the Anthroposophical Society') in which Rudolf Steiner's 'Letters to Members' and 'Anthroposophical Leading Thoughts' appear (CW 26). The next step is the creation of a new esoteric class, the 'first class' of the 'University of Spiritual Science' (which was to have been followed, had Rudolf Steiner lived longer, by two more advanced classes). Then comes a new language for Anthroposophy—practical, phenomenological, and direct; and Rudolf Steiner creates the model for the second Goetheanum. He begins the series of extensive 'karma' lectures (CW 235–40); and finally, responding to needs, he creates two new initiatives: biodynamic agriculture and curative education. After the middle of the year, rumours begin to circulate regarding Steiner's health. Lectures: January–February, *Anthroposophy* (CW 234); February: *Tone Eurythmy* (CW 278); June: *The Agriculture Course* (CW 327); June–July: *Speech Eurythmy* (CW 279); *Curative Education* (CW 317); August: (England, 'Second International Summer School'), *Initiation Consciousness: True and False Paths in Spiritual Investigation* (CW 243); September: *Pastoral Medicine* (CW 318). On September 26, for the first time, Rudolf Steiner cancels a lecture. On September 28, he gives his last lecture. On September 29, he withdraws to his studio in the carpenter's shop; now he is definitively ill. Cared for by Ita Wegman, he continues working, however, and writing the weekly installments of his *Autobiography* and *Letters to the Members/Leading Thoughts* (CW 26).

1925: Rudolf Steiner, while continuing to work, continues to weaken. He finishes *Extending Practical Medicine* (CW 27) with Ita Wegman.

On March 30, around ten in the morning, Rudolf Steiner dies

INDEX